TWAYNE'S WORLD LEADERS SERIES

Roy Wood Sellars

Courtesy of Bucknell University Press

Roy Wood Sellars

Roy Wood Sellars

W. PRESTON WARREN

Professor of Philosophy Emeritus
Bucknell University

TWAYNE PUBLISHERS

A DIVISON OF G. K. HALL & CO., BOSTON

Library of Congress Cataloging in Publication Data

Warren, William Preston, 1901-
Roy Wood Sellars.

(Twayne's world leaders series)
Bibliography: p. 135 - 42.
Includes index.
1. Sellars, Roy Wood, 1880 - 1973 2. Naturalism.
3. Realism.
B945.S424W37 191 74-30132
ISBN 0-8057-3719-1

MANUFACTURED IN THE UNITED STATES OF AMERICA

Contents

About the Author

Born at New Glasgow, Prince Edward Island, in 1901, William Preston Warren moved in 1919 with his widowed mother, two brothers and three sisters to the college town of Wolfville, Nova Scotia, where all attended Acadia University. Graduating cum laude with honors in economics, Preston studied philosophy and religion at Yale where he was Fogg Scholar for all three eligible terms and Day Fellow for the years 1927-29. Receiving his Ph.D. in 1929, he accepted an appointment in philosophy at Furman University. He spent the academic year of 1934-35 as General Education Board Fellow in Europe, at the universities of Berlin, Cambridge, and Prague. In 1942-43 he was visiting Professor of Philosophy at the University of North Carolina, and in 1945 he accepted the chairmanship of the Department of Philosophy at Bucknell University where he inaugurated the integrative university course program, notably strengthened his department, and taught until his retirement in 1971.

Dr. Warren's publications include:

Pantheism in Neo-Hegelian Thought, 3-28, Mennonite Press, 1931; later distributed by Yale University Press,

Masaryk's Democracy: A Philosophy of Scientific and Moral Culture, University of North Carolina Press, 1 - 254, 1941. (Also published by Allen & Unwin, London),

English version of Masaryk, T. G. *Ideals of Humanity*, Allen & Unwin, 1938. Now revised, with translator's Preface, as *Humanistic Ideals*, Bucknell University Press, 1970.

Principles of Emergent Realism: Essays by Roy Wood Sellars, with editor's Introductions and Foreward by Professor Sellars, Warren H. Green Inc., St. Louis, 1970.

Neglected Alternatives: Critical Essays by R. W. Sellars — with Editor's Preface, Bucknell University Press. 1973

Foreword

I have been asked to say a few words relevant to Professor Warren's treatment of my life and positions taken in philosophy. I think he has done a careful and well-documented account of my outlook. All I can add is a personal touch of confirmation and indications of background conditions and motivations.

I shall begin by saying that I was always in search of a general framework or perspective that would include answers to basic and perennial questions about man and his world. These seemed to me to be paramount and to be linked together in a fairly logical order.

First there was the question of human knowledge beginning with perceiving. I was persuaded that this question had not been approached in an open-minded enough way. Under the impact of the growth of natural science dominated by physics and astronomy, Cartesian dualism had expressed the consciousness of a sheer gulf between human life and the world around mankind. Man, as a result, was thrown back on himself; he was believed to be alien to nature. He had a soul or mind which set him apart from nature. I lived in an age already affected deeply by the notion of evolution, though it had not been clearly worked out.

Man like most animals is head-dominated, and his chief sense organs have the function of *guiding* him in his environment. Locke and his generation did not have a biological outlook but were dominated by one-way physics and Cartesian dualism. It is surprising how long this approach lasted.

A gull does not in the Lockian way apprehend his sensation and say, "What a beautiful sensation I have, but how can I get to the fish?" No, he looks through his visual sensation at the fish in the water. It is a one-step process usually called sensorimotor. Locke and others made it into a two-step operation and got puzzled over the second step, the copy or representation. Of course the gull did not *intuit* the fish. But he was concerned with it and guided by his eyes. As

I see it, man just developed [from the basis of] the gull's type of outlook and arrived at natural realism or commonsense realism, adding words and concepts. But hardly more than the gull did he understand perceiving as a complex operation. Looking at an object he still simply says: I *see it.* But I started to show that the mechanism involved the feeding in of information that referentially directed it while changing the information into *facts about the thing.* He never literally intuits the thing but starts to *know* it, that is, to have facts about it based on sensory information.

But philosophy had got puzzled and was divided between Berkeley's and Hume's sensationalism and the puzzling copy theory. Introspective psychology had no epistemology, and a man like James talked in terms of "percepts" taken in two contexts, instead of about perceiving. And Russell followed him in his so-called *neutral monism.* My colleague DeWitt Parker followed James in his radical empiricism. I stuck to analyzing the mechanism of perceiving. Behaviorism never had an epistemology. It just kept on with the biological outlook. My son Wilfrid says that Hume was puzzled but could not see how we could pass by inference to external things. He was not enough of a biologist in his era to see the circuit nature prepared. Russell at his best got into the brain but could not get out. Dewey gave up and resorted to "experiential behaviorism." The new realists lapsed into presentationalism. For them the only alternative was the rejected representationalism — Locke's second step. They simply changed Royce's cognitive relation into a negative relation. I rejected it entirely and said that we made things objects by responding to them and deciphering information received about them. But I could not retain natural realism's notion that we saw or intuited them. That is the essence of critical realism.

I think I was helped in all this by my course in the Main Concepts of Science, the first course of this kind which is so popular now.

To sum up, I found that I could not accept Locke's representationalism, nor Berkeley's resort to perceptual ideas as terminal, nor Hume's phenomenalistic sensationalism. I tended to take perceiving as involving an interplay of the percipient and the thing perceived. I finally arrived at the notion that this interplay involved a from-and-to circuit in which information was fed to the percipient to which he responded actively by way of translating this information in terms of thoughts about and words assigned in a social way. I realized that this process involved referential learning that was constantly being tested. Such learning is usually expressed as *facts about* the things perceived. These are elementary knowledge claims immersed in a largely sensuous thinking about the objects. This complex of activities is objectively directed but man has, as yet, no notion of its mechanism. He is, accordingly, inclined to believe that he just "sees" the thing before him. This would be a kind of action at a distance of which science had become skeptical. The job then was to show that such sensuous thinking was referentially directed to things outside the body and to break down the natural illusion that they were literally presented to the percipient. I sought to show that the *referential transcendence* was an achievement resting on stimulation — giving sensations — and directed response. There was no intuition at a distance but a referential claim.

Now this approach undercut, as Professor Warren has shown, the traditional idea of a cognitive relation of a unique sort between the percipient and the referential thing. I challenged this and challenged both Kant and the idealism founded by Hegel and Royce upon it. It also undercut representationalism with the two steps postulated by Locke, that is, the apprehended idea and its supposed counterpart, of which it was a copy. Incidentally, it undercut William James' radical empiricism that a percept is neutral and can be taken either in the context of a presented external world or in a personal and subjective context. As I have noted, my colleague Parker had adopted this scheme, as had Russell in his neutral monism.

Now all this was a growth which was only gradually clarified. It led, however, to a deeper consideration of the traditional mind-body problem. The first logical step was to challenge the mechanistic, dead-level notion of the physical world. I started this by advocating levels of casuality with organization. This later became the idea of emergence of novelty in nature, also adopted by Samuel Alexander and Lloyd Morgan. It is now usually discussed under the topic of a non-reductive view of life and mind. It is opposed to both mechanism and vitalism. Combined with my theory of perceiving, it led to my identity view of the brain-mind, a hyphenation which my friend J. B. Pratt did not like. I called this the double-knowledge, emergence approach to identity. We know the brain from outside, as the neurologists do, and yet are also on the inside as experiential participants in the brain's causal working.

This view logically led to what I called agential causality. In morality and all decision there is a guided working of the brain in terms of possible consequences of action and the allegiance to norms of conduct. Such agential causality went back to my idea in 1909 of levels of causality with organization. As I saw it, decision is an achievement influenced by education, personal experience, and reflection. Thus one's decision is not completely predetermined. This is equivalent to free will without appeal to a faculty called will. I grant conditioning but not in the behavioristic sense; it is non-reductive. I spoke of moral agential causality. As I saw it, science had not investigated the concept of agency.

I had long studied and pondered on religion as an explanation of man's condition and predicament. I wrote two books on the subject: *The Next Step in Religion* and *Religion Coming of Age*. Then, in 1933, I wrote *The Humanist Manifesto*. I had long been naturalistic in my outlook and had adopted the term "humanism" quite early. Man must stand on his own feet and try to solve his problems. I was aware of man's predicament and need for consolation and encouragement. It involved an adequate and sensitive philosophy of human life. I thought the age of appeal to special revelations was past. I wanted man to gentle himself and saw much good in Judaism, Christianity, Buddhism, and Islam, but their supernatural frameworks seemed to be outmoded. And they were too often motivated by dogmatism rather than by love and compassion. I did not aspire to be a militant founder of a new religion but the advocate of cultural growth and moral ecumenism.

I think that I have given the essentials of my philosophy with little concern with technicalities. These are in my many books and are well summarized by Professor Warren.

Thus far I have dealt largely with foundations. I wrote about social and political institutions and taught the corresponding subjects. But there are so many historical variables here. Perhaps the consideration of norms, such as justice, is the most fruitful. But changing technology is a great variable.

I close with some remarks on cosmology. In the ancient world there was the thought of a "great year" encompassing some ten thousand years or so. The old world was to go up in flames and a new world be formed. The earth was then considered the center of the universe.

Nietzche, a poet-philosopher of great erudition, was alarmed by the idea of eternal recurrence. He also had the idea of a superman. Biologists are now thinking of experimenting with man's gene pool.

As nearly as I can make out, the chief competitors today in cosmology are the "big bang" cycle theory and the "steady state" theory. Ours is a cosmos of super-galaxies and new discoveries are being made. Solar systems come and go and even galaxies. In this field philosophy can only reflect on scientific discoveries.

Conventional Christian wisdom speaks of special creation, and I find people hold that the universe had a beginning just like themselves. But is this not too much of an assumption? Aristotle held that the universe was eternal, and this bothered Aquinas. Shall I leave it at that? To theists this sounds rational; to humanists, somewhat magical. I have never had the glimpse of an idea of what creation *ex nihilo* could be like. Philosophy these days must be integrated with science, not reduced to it. For there are problems about human knowing and valuing. Science does not claim to be infallible; nor does philosophy. They are both growths in human culture.

In this regard, I should like to add an illustration from the semantics of relativity, a subject that had concerned me for many years.* Professor Tolland, who translated Einstein's first paper [on relativity], introduced me to the topic quite early. As I look back, I can see that what bothered me was, first, Einstein's emphasis on the term "relativity" with his use of observers in the bodies in "relative motion" and his omission of ordinary inertial motion; and, secondly, his contrasting use of the term "absolute motion" without clear indication of what he meant by it. I had already given up Newtonian space filled with ether as held by Lorentz. It almost seemed that Einstein recognized only "relative motion" with observers. I, on the other hand, as an empirical realist, took kinematics as motion in a straight line following acceleration, as when one throws a ball to another. Perhaps the idealists' claim that Einstein's appeal to observers favored their position affected me.

My first effort was to understand "relative motion," which I remember bothered A. O. Lovejoy also. I finally comprehended the setup involved. If two bodies are *separating* in a uniform way, each having observers on them, each can momentarily consider himself "at rest" and the other body in motion. This involves a pattern in which light can be used to chase the rod in motion. Einstein's denial of absolute simultaneity of light events on the two rods followed,

*The statement which follows is an abridged combination of three statements sent to the author successively by Professor Sellars to fill out and modify his previous remarks. There are, in consequence, likely to be distortions. — W.P.W.

since the light had to chase the body "in motion." Much was made of this lack of simultaneity in the two frames. It was a scheme and not an experiment.

It seemed to me that *the basic fact was the separating of the two bodies.* The scheme itself seemed to me justifiable and ingenious, but somewhat artificial.

Therefore I applied the same pattern to what I thought of as *relational motion.* If you accelerate one rod and not the one beside it, you will have the *same pattern* without special observers. It will be asymmetrical and light can be used to chase the rod which has been accelerated.

Poincaré had suggested that mass increases with velocity and the new physics was developed by Einstein on this basis.

Now I understand that physicists seldom use the relativity scheme in their physics — but could do so in exceptional circumstances.

My suggestion was that the term "relativity" befogged people. "Relational motion" was the ordinary kind. I recognized, of course, the use of light *in dating* distant events. But I had a hunch that simultaneous events meant actual events, actual as against past or future events. Of course, dating them was a technical job. Light is ordinarily employed to give a lapse to time within which the date is tentatively set.

Now I can sum all this up quite simply. Einstein neglected inertial motion of light and bodies because he was attacking absolute motion in Newtonian Space or Lorentz's ether. Hence he neglected (or so it seemed to me) asymmetrical *relational motion,* and puzzled people. His scheme was relevant to the struggle against absolute motion. But it neglected ordinary relational motion. *I was not attacking Einstein's physics* but *qualifying his emphasis on "relative motion" with observers.* It is largely a question of semantics. [See note 26, Chapter One]

Since writing the above at ninety-two, I have been reading Einstein's own account of the development of his theory and find it illuminating. I still think that he was bothered by Newtonian absolute time, that he came to the issue from a background of Ernst Mach's phenomenalism, and that there is much to be said for my definition of simultaneity in terms of co-actual events. But within his [Einstein's] framework, I wish now to express my full agreement with the theory of relativity. As I look back, I see that I did not appreciate Einstein's use of coordinate systems and his adoption of

Lorentz's transformation of Clerk-Maxwell's equations for light. Had I done so, I would have recognized the shift from Newton's outlook to the primacy of electro-magnetism.

I had always rejected Newtonian absolute time, which Einstein was also attacking. Happenings or events — the essence of time — seemed to me always to have a physical locus. Here I was on the right track. But I did not see clearly that inertial systems moving uniformly created a new problem. It was this circumstance that Einstein emphasized. He showed that one could not synchronize clocks moving rapidly on two different inertial systems — say, at 10,000 miles a minute — with respect to one another. He also had the difficulty of correlating simultaneous events in an inertial system — an embankment for instance, with a railway carriage moving uniformly along the embankment. I had been caught up in the literature of relativity but had not read Einstein's own book sufficiently. So I find that I was partly right yet also partly wrong.

When Einstein generalized to include gravitation, everyone admired his calculation of the amount of bending of the light. Let me express my admiration for him. The year of 1905 was his flowering. I wish that I could take the space to discuss our agreements and differences fully.

As I have indicated, I am now past ninety-two and no longer much concerned with recognition. I shall add a few words on genealogy and family life. I am a Canadian by birth but educated in the U.S.A. Through my mother I am a Stanley by descent. One of my ancestors in that line was Lord Lieutenant of Ireland under Queen Elizabeth I. Another appears in Shakespeare's *Richard III*. I am rather proud of the latter. My great-grandfather, David Wood, after whom I was named, was a captain under Brock in the battle of Queenstown Heights. He was educated in Edinburgh and became a patron of Queen's University in Kingston, Ontario. Thus I am not a Yankee like Dewey. But I am, and have always been, an internationalist in outlook. Neither Canada nor the Ivy colleges in the United States particularly recognized me. I flatter myself I was too original, and perhaps, radical. I was raised in a country village where my father was a doctor and druggist and justice of the peace. I had a happy home and skated and swam. I was in the Thumb of Michigan and there were many Canadians there. I graduated from what is now Ferris State College, had a quiet academic career, and a wonderful wife who was my cousin. She shared my genealogy but was also descended from a Scots doctor in the court of Catherine the Great of Russia. She had great skill as a translator of books from French. Needless to say, her death was a great blow to me.

I want, finally, to express my gratitude to Professor Warren for his insights and his excellent presentation of my thought.

Roy Wood Sellars

Ann Arbor

Preface

I have been privileged to prepare this book in consultation with Professor Sellars, who wrote the Foreword a few months before he died in 1973. He had in 1965 invited me to edit a series of his papers. The series later divided into two groupings: one volume — a cross section of his constructive thinking — was published in St. Louis in 1970 by Warren H. Green. A second volume of primarily critical essays was released by Bucknell University Press in 1973. Sellars himself, though 92, compiled a third volume of residual papers.

I have undertaken the task of placing Roy Wood Sellars in the perspective of great American thinkers. His contribution to American philosophy and his philosophical stature are becoming increasingly appreciated. This volume is directed to the presentation of his philosophy in the full range of its development.

Independent thinking is not born of following the patterns of others, be they Jameses, Royces, Deweys, Moores, Carnaps, Whiteheads, or Heideggers. Exploring the thinking of outstanding philosophers is indeed a part of the philosophical process, but not the adoption of one philosopher to the exclusion of others. Professor Sellars has not been that kind of thinker. He belongs with those who open up perspectives and, amid these, he compares favorably with the most notable. I have developed this theme in two statements: "Foundations of Philosophy" in the *Bucknell Review* (19, No. 3, 1971) and "Crossing the Philosophical Divides," the Roy Wood Sellars Lecture at Bucknell University, April, 1971. In the former I deal with Sellars in contrast with Dewey, Whitehead, and Heidegger. In the latter I treat Sellars' contributions to four problems that constitute philosophical divides: (1) that between the mind and the external world; (2) that between the non-living and the intelligently living; (3) that between the body and mind; and (4) that between individual wishes and social necessities. Sellars emerges not merely as a rugged pathmaker but as an elaborator of interrelated theories who has lived long enough to refine and amplify his insights. The result is a perspective that harmonizes our workaday conceptions with our more erudite reflections. Sellars' philosophy, accordingly, has basic components to offer to any other perspective.

Professor Sellars was laudatory of my work in some of the following chapters. He offered explanations and constructive comments on others. Overall he seemed to regard me as a particularly sympathetic expositor of his philosophy, though I must confess that my understanding of his work is no youthful adulation: I have written this volume following my retirement at seventy. I hope to have been guilty of an utter minimum of distortion.

W. PRESTON WARREN

Bucknell University

Acknowledgments

My greatest indebtedness is to the subject of this volume, Professor Roy Wood Sellars. Without his continuing participation by letter, the manuscript would be quite incomplete. I am also indebted to one of the co-editors of this series, Professor Thomas S. Knight, who read a draft of the manuscript and offered essential suggestions. My recent colleague Professor Joseph P. Fell has also read the manuscript, proposed stylistic changes, and raised questions toward sharpening meanings. Mrs. Carroll D. Weaver, former secretary of the Department of Philosophy, Bucknell University, has typed the entire manuscript, some of it three times.

I wish further to acknowledge my obligation to the publishers of Sellars' works, especially to the publishers from whom I have received permission to quote. These include: The Aristotelian Society for permission to quote from Roy Wood Sellars, "The Double Knowledge Approach to the Mind-Body Problem," *The Aristotelian Society Proceedings*, NS 23 (1923); the Aurora Press, from *Social Patterns and Political Horizons* (Nashville: Aurora Press, 1970); *Ethics*, from "Can a Reformed Materialism Do Justice to Values," *Ethics*, 55 (1944); *The Journal of Philosophy*, from "Critical Realism and the Time Problem," *Journal of Philosophy, Psychology and Scientific Methods*, 5 (1908), and "Causality," *Journal of Philosophy, Psychology, and Scientific Methods*, 6 (1909); *Mind* from "Sensations as Guides to Perceiving," *Mind*, 68 (1959); Pageant Press International Corporation, from *Principles, Perspectives, and Problems of Philosophy* (New York: Pageant Press, 1970); *Philosophy and Phenomenological Research*, from "Levels of Causality: the Emergence of Guidance and Reason in Nature," *Philosophy and Phenomenological Research*, 20 (1959) and "Existentialism, Realistic Empiricism, and Materialism," *Philosophy and Phenomenological Research*, 25 (1965); *The Philosophical*

Review, from "Why Naturalism and Not Materialism," *Philosophical Review*, 36 (1927) "The Analytic Approach to the Mind-Body Problem," *Philosophical Review*, 47 (1938), and "Causality and Substance," *Philosophical Review*, 52 (1943); "Reformed Materialism and Intrinsic Endurance," *Philosophical Review*, 53 (1944); Russell and Russell, from *Critical Realism: A Study of the Nature and Conditions of Knowledge* [1916] (New York: Russell and Russell, 1969); *Evolutionary Naturalism* [1922] reprinted with a new Preface by T. A. Goudge and an Appendix by Lloyd Morgan (New York: Russell and Russell, 1969); *The Philosophy of Physical Realism*, reprinted with two new chapters (New York: Russell and Russell, 1966); *The Humanist*, from "Humanist Manifesto," *The New Humanist*, 6 (1933); The University of Notre Dame Press, from *Reflections on American Philosophy from Within* (Notre Dame: University Press, 1969).

Chronology

1880 Born July 9 in Seaforth, Ontario, Canada, the son of Ford Wylis and Mary Stalker Sellars.

1884 Family emigrated to Pinnebog in mid-Michigan where father established medical practice.

1897 Entered Ferris Institute, Big Rapids, Michigan.

1898 Taught school.

1899 Entered University of Michigan.

1900 Had his first course in philosophy and was much stimulated.

1903 Graduated from the University of Michigan.

1903 - 1904 Attended Hartford Theological Seminary.

1904 - 1905 Teaching Fellow at the University of Wisconsin, working with F. C. Sharp.

1905 - 1906 Taught at University of Michigan on visiting appointment during Robert M. Wenley's leave of absence.

1906 Given continuing appointment at University of Michigan.

1909 - 1910 Studied in Europe, visiting Bergson, Husserl, Driesch and others.

1910 Instituted course in the Main Concepts of Science at University of Michigan.

1911 Married Helen Maud Stalker. Their issue, two children: Wilfrid S. and Cecily.

1916 Published *Critical Realism* and *The Next Step in Democracy.*

1917 Published *Essentials of Logic* and *Essentials of Philosophy.*

1918 Elected Vice President of the Eastern Division of the American Philosophical Association. Published *The Next Step in Religion.*

1920 Co-authored *Essays in Critical Realism.*

1921 Read paper in French to French Philosophical Society.

1922 Published *Evolutionary Naturalism.* Presented Paper before Aristotelian Society in London. Visited Bernard

	Bosanquet, James Ward, and Samuel Alexander.
1923	Elected President of the Western Division of the American Philosophical Association.
1926	Published *Principles and Problems of Philosophy.*
1928	Published *Religion Coming of Age.*
1930	Visited Samuel Alexander, G. E. Moore in England.
1932	Published *The Philosophy of Physical Realism.*
1933	Drafted *The Humanist Manifesto.*
1937	Toured Europe, visiting C. S. Strong in Fiesole, Italy.
1942 - 1946	Elaborated a Reformed Materialism in a series of essays.
1944	Debated in *Journal of Philosophy* with Sidney Hook.
1949	Co-edited with V. J. McGill and Marvin Farber *Philosophy for the Future: Quest of Modern Materialism.* Also contributed two essays.
1950	Retired as Professor of Philosophy, University of Michigan. Moved to Port Ryerse, Ontario (summers) and New York City (winters). Began revision of manuscript on social and political philosophy and restatement of basic positions, e.g., on perception.
1954	Honored by Symposium in *Philosophy and Phenomenological Research.* Daughter Cecily killed in auto accident
1962	Wife, Helen Maud Stalker Sellars, died. Moved back to Ann Arbor. Speaker at Philosophy Club of Yale University.
1963	Gave lectures at Bucknell University and University of Pennsylvania.
1965	Gave lectures at the University of New York at Buffalo and Syracuse University.
1966	Travelled three weeks in Russia.
1967	Travelled three weeks in England.
1968	Published *Lending a Hand to Hylas.*
1969	Published *Reflections on American Philosophy from Within.*
1970	Published *Principles, Perspectives and Problems of Philosophy* and *Social Patterns and Political Horizons.* Honored by Symposium at Notre Dame University.
1971	Gave lecture at Queens University, Kingston, Ontario.
1972	Attended Roy Wood Sellars lecture given by his son, Wilfrid at Bucknell University, April 16.
1973	Received degree of Doctor of Laws from Ferris State Technical School, successor to Ferris Institute attended in 1897 - 98. Died September 5 of a massive stroke.

CHAPTER 1

Biographically: Roy Wood Sellars

ORIGINATOR of critical realism, emergent evolutionist anteceding Lloyd Morgan and Samuel Alexander, proponent of a double knowledge and identity theory of the brain-mind relationship, and original American writer on religious humanism and drafter of the Humanist Manifesto, Roy Wood Sellars was born in Seaforth, Ontario, in 1880. The second son of Ford Wylis and Mary Stalker Sellars, he had a notable, predominantly Scottish ancestry. The Sellars came originally from the Glasgow region of Scotland, migrating first to Nova Scotia and then to Upper Canada (Ontario). They married into the distinguished Wood family.

Roy's great-grandfather, David Wood, after whom he was named, emigrated in the 1790's from Edinburgh, Scotland, where he was born and educated. He fought with distinction as a captain with Brock at Queenstown Heights in the War of 1812. He then became a successful industrialist in Nanticoke, southern Ontario, owning both a woolen and a lumber mill. Socially a squire, he also became a patron of Queens University at Kingston, Ontario.

On Roy's mother's side, the Stalkers were members of the Stuart clan with its royal tartan. They emigrated to York (later Toronto). A genealogy of the Stanleys in 1943 by Earl Spencer Armitage-Seeli Stanley of Lucan, Ontario, traces the Ontario Stanleys to Robert Stanleigh vel Stoneleigh who was sheriff of Lancashire in 1123 - 28. Robert Stanleigh, in turn, is shown to be the great-grandson of William, Count of Arques and great-grandson of Richard II, Duke of Normandy, a descendant of earlier royalty. R. W. Sellars writes: "I think I am proudest of the fact that an ancestor of mine, Lord Stanley, appears in Bosworth Field in Shakespeare's *Richard III*."[1]

Roy's father, as he has repeatedly said, was a "remarkable" man. He had been a teacher and principal in Seaforth, Ontario, where all three of his children were born. With this young family, one of them a baby, he set out for the University of Michigan Medical School and took his M.D. degree with one of the Mayo brothers in 1883. After a brief trial at medical practice in Detroit, he moved to Pinnebog, northern Michigan, in the thumb between Lake Huron and Saginaw Bay, where he would not have to wait for patients. Here he functioned not only as a medical doctor, but also became a druggist and justice of the peace. Between times, as an erstwhile educator, he tutored all three of his children.

Roy grew up quite happily in very rural Pinnebog with much outdoor life: skating, swimming, playing baseball and tending the garden. There were Norwegian, Anglo-Canadian and French Canadian boys. "It was a rather egalitarian situation . . . religious differences were taken for granted and ignored." A two-culture background disposed him to be international in outlook.

Although he had friends in the village and countryside, he had no intellectual competitors. He went to the village school; and on completion of the eight grades at Pinnebog, he was sent to the Ferris Institute at Big Rapids to prepare him for the university. "There," he said, "I began to stand out and gained the friendship of both Mr. and Mrs. Ferris." W. D. Henderson, his teacher in physics and chemistry, once visited Sellars's home and saw his father's library. "Now I know," he said, "why Sellars has stood out."[2]

The Ferrises in turn gave Roy the run of their private library. Here he found and read Edward Bellamy's *Looking Backward*, following this later with Morris's *News from Nowhere* and John Ball's *Dream*. The result was a critical attitude toward nation-states and wars. "The Spanish-American War was on," he said, "and I became skeptical of it. . . . I remember that some of the students drilled, but I did not."

A year at the Ferris Institute prepared him for the university, but he taught a rural one-room school for a year — all eight grades — and had more pupils than usual pass the county examinations. He himself passed an examination for a first-class lifetime teaching certificate. Earning twenty-eight dollars a month, he saved most of it.

Roy entered the University of Michigan in 1899. He washed dishes for his board during his first year, and then, with his brother, cooked his own meals. He states that he was not well prepared for the university, yet his selection of courses threw him in with the class ahead of him. Still, he says, he "made a go of it," so much so indeed that on graduation his class voted him one of the two most scholarly of its members. This opinion was evidently shared by Professor

Wenley of the philosophy department, who recommended him for a fellowship at the University of Wisconsin, and then invited him back to teach at Michigan while he himself was on sabbatical leave.

Roy took philosophy in his second undergraduate year. The department had gained status under Sylvester Morris and John Dewey. The latter had left for Chicago in 1896, three years prior to Roy's arrival. Robert M. Wenley, a Scotsman from Glasgow and a student of the Cairds (Edward and John) had been brought in to head the department. Other members in 1900 included Alfred H. Lloyd, a Harvard graduate who had studied in Berlin and later became dean of the graduate school and acting president. George Rebec was a third philosopher, a ready speaker who left in 1907 and later became prominent at the University of Oregon.

Sellars studied first with Wenley and found himself much attracted to philosophy. It "awakened me intellectually," he wrote in 1930, "and gave me perspective."[3] Sellars had earlier studied rhetoric under an effective teacher and had been impressed with Milton's power of able repetition. He also studied mathematics, going as far as calculus. In his senior year he took Hebrew under Craig and developed a critical, historically cultural approach to religion.

"I was shown," he said, "that the prophets were not foretellers, but speakers out of their conviction. It was early Christianity which sought in them the foretelling of Jesus as a Messiah. As the years went by, I got an historical perspective on Judaism. It had faith and trust, but neither a theology nor a philosophy. I remember Swinburne's lines 'we thank with brief rejoicing whatever cos [cause] there be that no man lives forever, that dead men rise up never, that even the longest river flows safely to the sea.' "

The idea of a science of religion was in the air, and Sellars accepted a scholarship at Hartford Theological Seminary for the academic year 1903 - 1904. There he came under a superb Arabist, Duncan Black MacDonald, and read the Koran in the original. The class discussed the great period of Arab culture with its stress on divine fore-ordination. Roy also studied New Testament Greek and thus began to have the languages of three cultures at his disposal. His education had thereby taken on a broad, yet fundamental, form.

In 1904 he was offered a teaching fellowship in philosophy at the University of Wisconsin. He spent a year at Wisconsin, studying under Sharp and Jastrow, conferring with Bode who was turning from Cornell's objective idealism to pragmatism, and associating with Max Otto and others. He worked through Stout's *Analytic*

Psychology in a seminar with Sharp. This was to be typical of Sellars: he was not oriented primarily in terms of James and Royce. There was, therefore, more independence to his thinking and a broader context.

Then another piece of luck came to him. Wenley, who was going on leave, asked Sellars to substitute for him in 1905 - 1906. The salary was eight hundred dollars, but Sellars did so substantial a job that he was asked to remain at Michigan at a beginning salary of nine hundred dollars. He was to continue at Michigan for forty-five years, at first with increments to his salary of one hundred dollars a year. It was not until 1911, when he was thirty-one and his salary was thirteen hundred dollars, that he could afford to marry.

Sellars spent the summer term of 1906 at the University of Chicago. Dewey was teaching experimental logic during the regular session, and Sellars worked with J. M. Baldwin. He wrote an essay in Baldwin's seminar on the mind-body relationship, pointing out a neglected alternative to Baldwin's theory. (The quest of neglected alternatives was to demark Sellars work throughout his professional life.) Baldwin had distinguished three possible progressions in the development of the mind-body complex. Anticipating his later identity theory, Sellars distinguished a fourth progression in the relationship of mind and brain, and in 1907 Baldwin published Sellars' essay in his *Psychological Review*. In 1908 Baldwin published two briefer papers by Sellars on "Consciousness and Conservation," and "An Important Antinomy." And in 1909, Baldwin was to give Sellars letters of introduction to Bergson, Boutroux, and Janet.

John Broadus Watson, the originator of behaviorist psychology, was also a graduate student who conferred with Baldwin. Hence Sellars had some direct contact with the primary source of behaviorism. A similar contact was to continue for many years at the University of Michigan. In his bachelor years, indeed, he roomed in the same house as the behaviorist John Shepard, and throughout his active life he kept close contacts with psychologists.

In 1908 Sellars took his doctorate at the University of Michigan with a thesis on the categories. He published essays on special categories over thirty-four years. His work on the categories, indeed, was to provide the basis for an epochal volume on *Evolutionary Naturalism*. To him, categories were not fixed ideas but concepts which emerged, developed, and became refined in the give-and-take of human activities.

He minored in sociology with Charles Horton Cooley. "We became friendly in after years," Sellars wrote, "and took walks together, talking about all sorts of topics. He was a very able man, somewhat of a social psychologist."

It is very interesting, however, that Wenley, who had earlier treated Sellars as his best student, did not approve Sellars' thesis for publication by the University. It was, Sellars thought, "too far from his idealism." Mrs. Carus, who later visited Alfred Lloyd in Ann Arbor, helped Sellars surmount this impasse by proposing to publish several of the chapters in *The Monist* and then to have the Open Court Publishing Company publish the book as a whole. The result was to be *Evolutionary Naturalism* (1922). Sellars had already published a number of essays on special categories in the *Journal of Philosophy* (1908, 1909, 1915).

Meantime, in 1916, Sellars published a volume on *Critical Realism,* developing a strand of thought that he had initiated in two articles in 1908.[4] This was a basic strand of his thought which gained him immediate distinction and which he continued to elaborate over more than fifty years.

The academic year of 1909 - 1910 Sellars spent in Europe. We have already mentioned his letters of introduction to Bergson and Boutroux. Sellars discussed with Bergson the possibility of a naturalistic emergent type of evolution. But Bergson referred him to the scientifically trained vitalist, Hans Driesch, with whom he then studied in Heidelberg. Sellars' recollections of Driesch are not indicated in his records; but he did have personal discussions with him, and there seems little doubt that Driesch pointed him to relevant specifics in physiology.

At Heidelberg, he also conferred with Windelband. In France he had had conversations with Boutroux and Janet. About his conference with Boutroux, who stressed the contingency of laws of nature, Sellars said: "It was not a long conversation." But the idea of levels of causality gained an increment from positions such as Boutroux's.

Sellars returned to teaching with a notable course in the philosophy of science. It focussed on the "Main Concepts of Science." "We sometimes used Ward's *Naturalism and Agnosticism,* but also read Huxley, Mach, Poincaré, and Pearson," Sellars recalled. Many of his students were graduate students in physics, chemistry, and biology. "I learned much from them," he has written. They studied perceiving, scientific method, possible evolutionary levels in nature, and the mind-body problem. All this found expression in his *Critical Realism* and his *Evolutionary Naturalism*.

Three important developments had meanwhile occurred. In 1911 he married his cousin, Helen Maud Stalker, an intelligent and beautiful woman who was a great helpmate until her death in 1962. In the early years of their marriage, Helen translated Bouglé's *Evolution of Values* for which Roy wrote a preface.[5] In 1912 and 1913 their two children were born: Wilfrid, who was to become a most eminent philosopher, and Cecily who became a minister's wife and a psychologist.

In 1916, Sellars, who had begun teaching social philosophy along with his other courses, published *The Next Step in Democracy*. This book argued in the name of socialism for adequate concern for human welfare as well as for business success. Published a year before the Russian revolution, the volume envisioned a gradual social transformation of society. Sellars' interest in the social order, we have noted, went back to his reading of Bellamy, Morris, and Ball. His social questioning began in principle still earlier: in a childhood experience of a political rally in a tent on the river flats near his home.

"Of course," he wrote years later, "I did not know what it was all about, but there was singing and snatches of one song remain with me:

> The ship is coming round the bend,
> It's all loaded with Harrison men.
> Goodbye Grover, goodbye oh,
> What makes you cry so?"[6]

His social concern gained force from the progressivism of LaFollette during Roy's year in Wisconsin. As we shall show in Chapter 7, social philosophy became indeed the crowning or completion of his thinking.

In 1918 Sellars published another "next step." This time it was *The Next Step in Religion*. The next step in religion was an outright humanism. According to Sellars, religious thought historically has been prescientic and hence mythopoetic. The time had arrived for a religion which comes to terms with the world disclosed through science. The universe of science shows no evidence of being deiform, but it does hold human values which should be cherished by both the individual and society; and it does present the option of living from the viewpoint of the whole and the long run, and this is what constitutes religion. Let men therefore live as citizens of a world to be made the most of.

Sellars' socio-cultural approach to religion grew out of his study of languages and the cultures they articulated: Hebrew, Arabic, and Greek. As he saw it, the era of modern science brings utterly different perspectives than those that gave form to the historic religions.

In 1922, Sellars published his *Evolutionary Naturalism*. The Major content of this book went back to his doctoral thesis. It was an epochal publication. Both Lloyd Morgan's *Emergent Evolution* and Samuel Alexander's first statement of emergent evolution were published a year later.[7] Morgan added an appendix to his volume, distinguishing his position from that of Sellars. "Mine," said the latter, "was more systematically empirical and naturalistic." There was no introduction of a mysterious nisus or or extra-natural control. Material organization was the key concept. Morgan told Sellars that to his knowledge, he (Sellars) was the first to publish on emergent evolution.

In that same year Sellars presented a paper to the Aristotelian Society in London; his subject was "The Double Knowledge Approach to the Mind-Body Problem." The invitation to give such a paper came from the secretary of the society, H. Wildon Carr. "Carr was pleasant to me at my lecture," Sellars recalled, "but I had the feeling that others hardly knew what I was driving at. . . . Russell and Moore dominated the [English] field."[8]

Sellars had read a similar paper in French before the French Philosophical Society a year earlier. It is interesting that Sellars did not get comparable invitations in the United States. Like the Lowells and Cabots of the New England tradition, the Ivy League east was quite self-contained.

On his trip to Britain, Sellars stayed at the home of James Ward, whose *Naturalism and Agnosticism* he had used in his course on the Main Concepts of Science. "We played a game of chess and Dawes Hicks visited us," Sellars wrote in a letter of February 5, 1973. "I have been told that his [Ward's] annotated copy of my *Critical Realism* went to either Birmingham or Manchester . . . He took me one night to Trinity high table where I met Lord Rutherford and others."

Sellars wrote also concerning Samuel Alexander: "He asked me to visit him and I did so and greatly enjoyed it. One objection that he made to my critical realism was that it implied that his realism was naïve. I hastened to deny this; I thought it very sophisticated. I was opposing natural or commonsense realism, with its assumption that one intuited the object. He [Alexander] was a delightful person. I met him again in 1930 at the International meeting in Oxford, and we got along beautifully together."

It was Samuel Alexander who called the attention of both Lloyd Morgan and A. N. Whitehead to Sellars' *Evolutionary Naturalism*. Whitehead, however, was too committed a theist, and, indeed, too much of a philosophical idealist and mathematical artist to find emergent naturalism congenial. The conception of a cosmic artist was more to his intellectual taste.

The following year, 1923, Sellars was elected president of the western division of the American Philosophical Association. His address on "The Emergence of Naturalism" he later described as "largely a literary production," but the fact that it was praised by the philosopher of science, Herbert Feigl, speaks for its cogency and substantiality.

Just as relevant for Sellars' biography was the publication in that same year of an article on "Critical Realism and its Critics." Four years had passed since the release of a collaborative volume of *Essays in Critical Realism*, and eight years since the appearance of his own *Critical Realism*. The publication of the latter volume had in fact brought Sellars prompt recognition. He had good reviews in *Revue Philosophique* and in *Mind*, and a notable statement in Woodbridge Riley's *American Thought*. Professor J. E. Creighton of Cornell University, who had read the *Critical Realism*, secured Sellars' election as vice president of the eastern division of the American Philosophical Association. And Durant Drake of Vassar visited Sellars to ask about the possibility of using the caption of 'Critical Realism' for a volume that a number of realists were projecting. Sellars was, as a matter of course, invited to participate. The result was a series of essays in critical realism by Durant Drake, A. O. Lovejoy, J. B. Pratt, A. K. Rogers, George Santayana, R. W. Sellars, and C. A. Strong.

It was specifically in response to this volume that the critics of critical realism were writing. Two misconceptions stood out for Sellars. The first was an assumption that a realistic theory must be intuitionist to be viable. Two of the critics, L. A. Reid and G. E. Moore, were intuitionists. Sellars believed that they were not sufficiently or correctly analytic. The critical realist is more analytic, distinguishing "more carefully between the conditions and instruments of knowledge and knowledge itself," he argued. The critical realist "examines the content . . . which mediates knowledge and reflectively distinguishes it from the object known by means of it."[9]

But how can we ever know that the content of knowledge, i.e., what we seem to know about a thing, actually discloses the thing? This was Turner's problem in "The Failure of Critical Realism."[10] Sellars' answer first disowns one strand that became associated with critical realism through the essays of Santayana, Drake, and Strong. He then proceeds to make a case for the objective referrals of content to things. (This is the key issue of our next chapter.) Yet the essay on "Critical Realism and its Critics" marks an important assessment of the problem for Sellars. His writing takes a fresh turn.

Now, in fact, begins the period of disentangling and developing essentials. It was a period of both consolidation and fresh elaboration. There were two lines of development in Sellars' philosophy: (1) from a professed epistemological dualism with a referential component to a direct referential realism; and (2) from a general physical naturalism to an outright reformed materialism. The latter development was slower in occurring and had indeed to await the appropriation of the term "naturalism" solely for a methodology — the methodology of science — but both developments were expressed in his 1932 opus, *The Philosophy of Physical Realism.* The title, indeed, was intended to convey the uniting of a realistic epistemology with a physicalist ontology. It may be that the referential theory of perception stands out more clearly in this work than the materialist "metaphysics," though the more incisive statements of the former were also to come later.[11] We shall treat each of these developments in Chapters 2 and 3, respectively; suffice it here to state that Sellars not only repudiated epistemological dualism in 1932, but that he repudiated dualisms of every other variety,[12] and he explicated the bio-functional mechanism of perception. He made it clear throughout, moreover, that his was a substantive, and not merely methodological, naturalism. He had scored his physicalism as early as 1913,[13] though he was unwilling as late as 1927 to call his ontology "materialism." By 1942, however, he had reversed his position and declared himself for an updated materialism.[14]

It would be difficult to weigh the factors in the refinement of Sellars' philosophy: the "isms" coming on the American scene —

positivism, Whiteheadeanism, existentialism; the work of such scientists as C. Judson Herrick, Lord Brain, Sherrington and others. Sellars' philosophy was refined vis-à-vis successive isms, but it was refined in the light of the findings of neurologists and other scientists, and the development of information and communication theories. His interchanges with Herrick are typical. They shared their respective ideas and exchanged manuscripts. We shall refer to this later in treating the mind-body problem. Association with psychologists and the feedback from other scientists were, moreover, not without impact. The zoologists H. S. Jennings and Emerson Ritter wrote to him following the publication of his *Evolutionary Naturalism*; also Wheeler at Harvard. "It seems strange indeed," Sellars has commented, "that I seemed to get more appreciation from American scientists than from American philosophers." European philosophers were more responsive.

Three other factors are selected here for attention because of their evident immediacy: Sellars' give-and-take with his colleague, DeWitt Parker, over forty years; his collaboration with Marvin Farber from 1940 on; and his exchanges with Sydney Hook in 1944.

A student at Harvard of Royce, James, Santayana, Palmer, Perry and Munsterberg, DeWitt Parker came to Michigan in 1908 to fill the vacancy left by Rebec, and except for two years at the University of California, he taught at Michigan until his death in 1949. An aesthetician distinctively, what Parker sought philosophically was "to bring Berkeley and Leibniz up to date in an empirical kind of monadism. He postulated an Omega system at the foundation of the monads." "I know of no one," Sellars continued, "who could develop a philosophy resting on an imaginative extension of the insights found in personal experience better than Parker . . . [and] he was sensitive to basic categories such as causality and substance. I flatter myself that his treatment of substance in his book *Experience and Substance* owed something to our continuing debates."[15]

It was a case of Philonous versus Hylas, except that Hylas was not as tractable as in the Berkeleyan dialogues. And each was highly appreciative of the other. Parker paid the notable tribute to Sellars that "No American has done more persistent and original thinking on the fundamental philosophical problems in the last thirty years or so than my colleague, Professor Sellars."[16] The latter has reciprocated at some length. "I could not have had a better colleague than Parker," he wrote. "While I was working out the scheme of evolution, levels and novelty, he was keeping me aware of the uniqueness of experience." And "he asked searching questions."[17]

The exchange with Hook came in the *Journal of Philosophy* in 1944. The debate began with a criticism of Hook's treatment of materialism in an article published some years before, though the immediate occasion of the criticism was the conception of naturalism pervading the recent publication of a symposium on *Naturalism and the Human Spirit*.[18] While he elaborated his statement in some thirty-four theses, the core of Sellars' proposal was that the conception of matter be revised to take account of emergent levels arising with degrees and types of organization. The organic self is one type of physical substance, but this is not to be construed as in any sense reductive. It is rather a revelation of the possibilities in the organization of matter.

Sellars' article had been entitled "Is Naturalism Enough?" Hook replied with a comparably questioning title: "Is Physical Realism Sufficient?"[19] He proceeded to show that it wasn't. There are other existences than physical existence. Sadness and joy are cases in point, though he did not claim that sadness and joy have any existence other than as states and/or processes of certain physical entities. Their distinguishability from the bodies which they characterize is operationally sufficient. What is common to the many varieties of naturalism and materialism is not a theory of stuff or of the constitution of matter, or a theory of knowledge, or an ontology, but the belief that valid knowledge is knowledge warranted by scientific method, and the confidence that the application of scientific method — not just a method of the techniques of physics — to all fields of human experience will enlarge our understanding or increase our control. As a consequence of this commitment, naturalists and materialists whenever they have the courage of their method, always find themselves in doctrinal opposition to idealists of all varieties on the question of the existence of God or the presence of Cosmic Purpose.[20]

It would probably not be too unkind to say that the debate has so far followed the party lines of the pragmatists and substantive realists. Now Sellars, while pointing out their areas of agreement, presses the issue of substance further. His response takes the form of another question: "Does Naturalism Need Ontology?" It would be more accurate to phrase it: but does *not* naturalism need ontology? There is something hazy and incomplete, indeed foundationless, about a naturalism that does not have its basis in substantial existents. The recognition of physical things in such a series as organisms, histories (of what?), and perspectives (on what?) is ambiguous. Hook's criticism of Sellars' use of terms could be turned on operational thinking *per se*. It assumes more than it proposes and brings in its unproclaimed baggage by a rear door. Operationalism of what? By what? For what? The "for what" is what is actually acknowledged. "Reformed Materialism and Intrinsic Endurance" is Sellars' most intensive statement on the issue of substantive existence.[21]

Sellars' relationships with Marvin Farber have been another factor in the advancement of his mature philosophy. On the editorial board of *Philosophy and Phenomenological Research* from its inception, Sellars not only had manuscripts to pass on, but he had a relatively ready forum for his own writing. At least a dozen of his papers have been published in *PPR*. As evidence of a kinship of viewpoint, moreover, Sellars, Farber, and McGill joined in a cooperative volume on *Philosophy For the Future* in 1949.[22]

Later, in a 1954 issue of *Philosophy and Phenomenological Research*, Farber published a symposium on Sellars' philosophy to which the latter wrote a rejoinder. One could say, indeed, that both Parker and Farber set a pattern of relationships with Sellars that were conducive to intensively productive work. Farber, further, sought out Sellars for lectures and symposia.[23] To a quite marked extent, however, Sellars worked alone, independently pursuing ideas that gave him occasion to ponder.

Sellars retired in 1950 from his teaching activities. Professor Morris Lazerowitz, a former student, writes that he still retains a vivid impression of him as an excellent teacher with high intellectual integrity, and as an original scholar, which showed itself even in his discussion of elementary topics. He sought out the better graduate students for discussions, not only because he was genuinely interested in an exchange of ideas, but because he wanted to make sure that he was keeping abreast of developments in fields other than his special one.

Lois Sharbach Garvin, another of Sellars' students, said: "I took only one course with Dr. Sellars. It was at the beginning of the war. I and about a hundred other students thought his idea for this course a smashing one, for it was a course in political philosophy and therefore something young people could focus on in those confusing times. It dealt with, if I remember rightly, democracy, socialism, communism, and fascism presented chronologically. I suppose that we all had the idea that the approach to these isms would be in some way propagandist. We were completely fooled. It was an approach which concerned itself first with the history and then the analysis of the theory of politics that each embodied. I remember no slanting, no emotionalism; only a good scholarly presentation of what he felt young people of that time should know. On me it had the effect of inducing the feeling that this was a person who had lived long enough to have seen much, saying to us: 'this is where we are now, but some day someone else will be talking in a different time about what happened then, and there will be a new and different political philosophy which will take us to other crises.' "

Professor Archie Bahm, a reader for a big introductory course in philosophy who later taught sections of the course and also prepared the index for Sellars' *Philosophy of Physical Realism*, is more general in his comments. He relates that Roy Wood and Mrs. Sellars "were interested in their students; they invited my wife and me over to dinner and an evening occasionally. He was always cordial and considerate . . . I agree with those who hold that he was not sufficiently appreciated by other philosophers. If you look at my *Philosophy, an Introduction*, you will see how Sellars' *Principles and Problems of Philosophy* had its influence, and how I developed further ideas." Sellars had challenging content and cogency in his teaching.

In 1954 a tragedy occurred in Sellars' life. His daughter, Cecily, a state psychologist in North Dakota, was killed in an auto accident. The repercussion from this tragedy affected Sellars' publications, though he remained an incessant scholarly writer. In his nineties, he was catching up with papers he had been working on at the time of the tragedy.

I had the privilege of helping Sellars pull out of a second tragedy, his wife's death in 1962. She has been characterized as a beautiful, intelligent, and sensitive woman. Her death, after fifty-one years of marital partnership, left a deep vacuum. It was after that second loss that I began a series of communications with him, issuing in his visit to Bucknell in 1963 and in continuous exchanges over the succeeding years. He returned at once to his writing and occasional lecturing, traveling to Florida, to Britain, and to Russia, and producing a volume of publications that few, certainly at that age, have equalled. His published writings in his eighties include two books and some dozen articles. He also prepared two major tomes, *Principles, Perspectives, and Problems of Philosophy* and *Social Patterns and Political Horizons*, that were issued when he was ninety. Both were the crystallization of many years teaching and writing. Three other books went through reprintings.[24]

He was also, in his nineties, much concerned with the semantics of the theory of relativity. As he has indicated in his Foreword, this is not a new development. He studied this theory in 1907 from a translation of Einstein's original statement. In 1932 he discussed the interpretation of relativity in a note under that title in the *Philosophical Review* and in three articles in 1946.[25] Believing that he had been misunderstood as an opponent of relativity physics, Sellars was concerned to restate his case not against the physics of relativity but against its semantics. Now he found, on rereading Einstein, that he was much more in agreement with him than he had thought. Still, he believed that there was need for a realistic statement of the issues.[26]

Notre Dame University has the distinction of providing a capstone to Sellars' career. In September, 1970, the Notre Dame Philosophy Department honored Sellars' ninetieth year with a symposium on his philosophy. The symposiasts included: Andew J. Reck of Tulane, Wilfrid Sellars of Pittsburgh, and C. F. Delaney of Notre Dame. [27] Having a son who is a philosopher with his own extension of his father's philosophy is the greatest of capstones. Professor Sellars died on September 5, 1973, leaving behind a distinguished body of writing and a distinguished son to keep the name of Sellars bright in the world of philosophy.

CHAPTER 2

Referential Critical Realism

SELLARS' first major contribution was his critical realism. Like Charles Peirce's *pragmatism,* the term *critical realism* was to be taken up in a few years and associated with better known men.[1] But unlike pragmatism, critical realism was not to be developed acceptably by most of its adopters.[2] It was Roy Wood Sellars who was not only the originator but the consistent developer of critical realism.

Critical realism is a theory of knowledge. Sellars' philosophy developed around a core of problems in epistemology, ontology, and the mind-body relationship. These problems were, for him, intimately interrelated. The disentangling of one of them for separate treatment, therefore, was like separating functions from the things that function. Still, it is quite possible to treat epistemology with a minimum of reference to the natures of the things that know and of those that are known. Sellars did this essentially in his *Critical Realism* (1916), and he did the converse in his *Evolutionary Naturalism* (1922). We shall follow him, accordingly, in focusing on his realism in this chapter and on his evolutionary, substantive naturalism in Chapter 3.

At the heart of critical realism is the problem of perceptual knowledge. For something that is so close to everyday action as perceiving is, its theoretical understanding has been a strangely difficult matter. The analyses by Berkeley, Hume, and even Schopenhauer in terms of perceptual images and ideas have had to be reckoned with and, if possible, surmounted. And no statement of a contrary position which does not account for their findings can claim adequacy. "Only a realism that passes through idealism can hold its ground,"[3] declares Sellars.

Yet common sense distinguishes ideas from the things of which they are ideas, and common sense has a considerable degree of success in everyday living. It deals in the relations of personal organisms to the things of their world, and it would seem that a theory of knowledge should account for knowledge of such rudimentary entities as those in the world of one's body.

But on what basis or in what terms can we account for knowledge of physical things? Are these directly present to consciousness? Do we intuit them? Or are the immediate objects of experience images and ideas? If so, can we infer external entities from them? Or is there some other basis on which we can claim knowledge of physical bodies?

These are questions around which realism was formulated and developed early in this century. One group, calling their view the "New Realism," banded themselves together in 1909 and published a "Program and First Platform of Six New Realists" in 1910.[4] In 1912 they published *The New Realism*.[5] Two of their contentions were that (1) "some at least of the *particulars* of which we are conscious exist when we are not conscious of them," and (2) "some at least of the particulars . . . that are real are apprehended directly rather than indirectly through copies or mental images."[6]

Here was a presentational realism, as contrasted with a representational, dualistic realism such as Locke's. But how explain this directness of perception? It is not enough to assert it as an intuition. Intuitions must justify themselves or otherwise be dogmas and contradicted by other intuitions.

Two of the new realists, E. B. Holt and R. B. Perry, were behaviorists in their psychology and advanced a theory of perceptual knowledge on the model of a searchlight. From this standpoint, consciousness is that portion of the environment to which the organism specifically responds. But how account for error and illusion on this thesis? Physical responses can be made to imagined as well as to real objects.

Later new realists[7] proposed an objective relativism according to which everything of which we are aware, whether hallucinatory or otherwise, is objective in its own way. But this led to the problem of distinguishing perspectives which are most reliable from those that are less reliable, and, among the latter, of recognizing those that are least reliable. It was a problem involving an "unmanageable complexity."[8]

Meantime other realists were attempting to find a more fruitful basis for perceptual knowledge. Sellars, who began writing on critical realism in 1908 — two years before the new realists published their "Program and First Platform" — did not write in the first instance against neo-realism. Critical realism was juxtaposed to, though built up from, common sense realism. This was said to be the realism of the "plain man": that attitude toward the world in which it is thought to be independent of the event of perceiving, but for which the problem of differences and discrepancies in perception has not yet fully arisen. When therefore Joseph Boodin treats critical realism as an arrogant assertion that the new realists were naïve he is not referring to the original meaning of critical realism.

I have mentioned Sellars' articles in 1908. He wrote two of them on "Critical Realism and the Time Problem." In the first article, he states that "critical realism, although it regards experience as characteristic of parts of our present world, viz., the nervous systems of men and animals, is not forced to assume that this was the case in the past." Anticipating his emergent naturalism, he continues: "qualitative changes in reality are quite possible." Implicit is the thought that things or beings may be developed through special organizations of matter that have the capacities for conscious experience. Reality is in process. Process indeed portrays "the dynamic character of reality. It signifies that 'to be' is 'to be active.' "[9]

In "Critical Realism and the Time Problem II," he makes a number of points: first, that an experience is always an individual's experience; there is no such thing as experience in general; second, that the relation of the individual's experience to the rest of him which we call his body, as a part of reality, is the "vital metaphysical problem and the key to critical realism." Third, the transcendence of experience is a pseudo-problem, declares Sellars: "The correct and illuminating questions are: What is the function of experience? What can it be expected to tell us of existences around the body. . . . I believe that experience tells us the function, structure, and relations of existences, and that in doing this it is not compelled to transcend itself."[10]

But experience can be critical or uncritical. We do not have to go to Kant to find the meaning of the term *critical.* There are different modes and levels of philosophical criticism. Natural realism is largely uncritical and unable to explain its own findings. Natural realism is, as we have said, the viewpoint of the plain man. The latter pictures a world of physical objects and believes that physical things are directly present in his field of vision. "Stars, rivers, mountains, tenements, street cars, books . . . are all considered objects which exist in a common world to which we must adapt ourselves," Sellars states.[11] There is a realistic structure to experience which in the first instance is mainly pictorial.

Critical realism is, *per contra,* tutored by science and critical thinking. It differs very considerably from natural realism, modifying the thinking of the plain man in the light of the findings of science. Scientific knowledge about the world consists of propositions which do not attempt to picture it. "Science offers us measurements of things and statements of their properties," says Sellars, ". . . their effects on us and upon other things, and of their structure, but it unconsciously swings over more completely away from the assumption that physical things are open to our inspection or that substitute copies [of them] are open to our inspection."[12] Scientific knowledge is not an intuition of the stuff of the physical world. What we obtain by intuition or observation of our own perceptual processes is psychical, i.e., images and ideas. This is the component of truth in the various idealisms; and for Sellars, as we have already quoted, only a realism which has surmounted idealism "can hold its ground."[13]

But can science provide such a realism? Its propositions "must be tested immanently or within experience," and they constitute "idea objects" rather than physical existents.[14] At its realistic best, must this not imply a duality of idea-objects and actual existing things? And how can we know the actual existents or that there are any entities beyond the contents of minds?

"Epistemological dualism," maintaining that the object of experience and the actual existent are two different things, is indeed a charge that was levelled at the critical realists. In his "Story of American Realism," Montague asserted that none of them had gone beyond Descartes and Locke.[15] It became common, in fact, to say that the new realists could not account for error but that the critical realists could not account for truth.

Sellars actually professed epistemological dualism in an essay on "Epistemological Dualism vs. Metaphysical Dualism,"[16] and I have attributed this to the first stage of his critical realism. But on further thought questions emerge as to what extent he was an epistemological dualist or whether he was actually an epistemological dualist at all. Scientific thinking (i.e., in physics, chemistry, biology, astronomy, geology) is about something other than itself and other than human experience as such. It is regarded as *tested knowledge* about "that which never can be literally present within the field of experience."[17] In Chapter 7 of *Critical Realism,* seven problems are developed in some detail to demonstrate the pressure within experience to accept an external control of experience and of a continuous medium within which minds live and have their being. "The thought of the physical world comes back," in consequence, "with renewed force."[18]

The meaning of knowledge is contained in fact in two components: first, the idea-object which takes form in propositions about something other than itself; and, secondly, the component or factor of reference. The structure of experience contains this dynamic element of referral to the sources of stimulation. This is particularly evident in the natural realism of the plain man. But it is also close to the surface in the thinking of many scientists. If you ask a scientist what table indeed he is judging about, he will usually reply, "The one I see in front of me."[19] This reply is not, however, meant to assert that he is intuiting a physical thing but that the physical thing is causally connected with his present thing-experience, and that there is a "one to one correspondence" between his thing-experience and the entity which controls it. This correspondence indeed is unique and is built around the body. Thus the mechanism of reference obtains within experience yet reaches beyond it.

The full import of this referential component belongs to the later stages of Sellars' realism, but there can be no question of his claim to be a referential rather than inferential realist. At this point, therefore, we should distinguish inferential realists from presentational realists, and referential realists from both. The neo-realists, we have said, were presentationalists. The critical realists, Montague said, were inferentialists.[20] In characterizing the epistemology of the critical realists, he wrote that "material things are only mediately known, being inferred as the direct or indirect causes of the ideas."[21] In this characterization Montague groups together all seven critical realists. Sellars, *per contra*, has contended that they were all in quest of a direct referential realism. How indeed infer material entities from ideas if one has not already had some intelligible acquaintance with material bodies? Suffice it here to emphasize, in any case, that Sellars was certainly in quest of a referential rather than either an inferential or presentational realism and that he made a preliminary case for a referential realism in the 1916 publication of his *Critical Realism*.

The *Critical Realism*, as we mentioned in Chapter 1, was followed in four years by a collaborative volume of essays by seven non-presentational realists. This group of seven, however, divided on the basis of their conceptions of perceptual knowledge. Drake, Santayana, and Strong held that what we are immediately aware of when we perceive anything is an *essence* or distinguishable something, such as a sense datum or mathematical element (line, point, angle), and that in veridical perception this essence corresponds to the essence of the object.[22] This, as Montague pointed out, *was* epistemologically dualistic, though the exponents alleviated their dualism by additional considerations. Santayana, for example, had a pragmatic element in his philosophy which enabled the referral of essences to entities to become relevant — or else!

Pratt, Lovejoy, and Rogers were not exponents of the perception of essences. They emphasized the *intentionality* of experience. Percepts normally refer to, intend, or otherwise designate things that are "not part of our mental content." The intentionality of perception was a conception that in modern times stemmed from the Austrian philosopher-psychologist Franz Brentano. For all three intentionalists, in consequence, there was an ultimate *mystique* about the intentionality of experience. But Sellars, who aligned himself with this sub-group, wrote that he believed that he "alone explored the biological base of perceiving"[23] and found its evolutionary function or role. It was Sellars who was able thereby to develop critical realism as a clearly referential realism.

Sellars' referential realism was developed in fact over five decades. We shall attempt to demark his recognition of its several ingredients. And, first of all, there is an essential ingredient from behavioristic psychology: the relation of physical response to perception. Evolutionarily, perception develops in the process of dealing with entities that threaten or assist organic existence. It is therefore built up around physical response. The reflex arc is, in fact, the type of pattern to which perceiving belongs: a from-and-to circuit or circuit of return. An organismic or wholist psychology will recognize this fact. Perceiving is thus a component of a more inclusive process and is not to be adequately understood apart from that process. Sellars develops this thesis in two books and a number of articles.

In the *Principles and Problems of Philosophy* (1926) Sellars first includes the from-and-to circuit as the structure in terms of which to understand perceiving. The unit in perceiving includes a stimulus or stimuli from an entity or entities, the organic production of sense data consequent on the stimulation, and an organic referral to the source of the stimulus. "What is that?" or, "Is that the baby?" are typical responses to sounds. It requires a very considerable sophistication to treat sounds simply as essences. They are, in the first place, signs or evidences of things. I recall my daughter at three years of age saying in a guttural voice for the birds, "The tide is out; my fish are here." Many birds do not have to wait for the ebb tide. The gannet dives down directly from the surface to catch its fish and similarly, the hawk from the air, for its land prey. Humans develop symbols and processes of reflection. But they are basically, in the first instance, dealing with things (in situations) which affect their existence favorably or adversely. Sensations are not characteristically objects of perception but signs and disclosures of things.

In his major opus, *The Philosophy of Physical Realism*, Sellars undertakes to round out his theory of perceptual knowledge in terms of six principles. These principles are:

1) Human knowing is conditioned in a perfectly natural way in regard to both external controls and internal operations. This involves both the sources and circumstances of the stimulus and the response of the organic recipient to the object. The response is coordinated and relevant. The great mistake of seventeenth-century philosophy was to ignore the response-component of perception.

2) Though causally conditioned and resting on neuromuscular mechanisms, human knowing is no less knowing. To deny that we know because knowing has natural conditions is like saying that we cannot see because we must see with our eyes. Human knowing is an achievement and, like all achievements, rests on abilities and tools.

3) The causal theory of perceiving should be restated as the causal theory of sense data. It is only slowly that psychologists and philosophers have learned to grant that our perceptual experiences are organizational and responsive. They have viewed them as too completely passive and atomistic. Perceivings are more than the having of sense data; they involve reference and predication. And predication requires conceptualization.

4) Knowing must be studied at its various levels as a characteristic claim of the knower. In perceptual knowing, one gives predicative meaning to the visual datum, but sense cognition is neither arbitrary nor a matter of animal faith. Knowing is a claim which must pass tests. It is things in the external world that elicit and control our interpretation of them.

5) The act of cognition is complex and appears in consciousness as an interpretation of an external object in terms of rational conceptions. It is distinctive of critical realism that perceptual knowing is a critically reflective process in which categories are employed. The

critical realist asserts that the very organic activity of perceiving — with its polarity which stimuli elicit — founds a structured consciousness replete with meanings and directions, affirmations and contrasts.

6) Things are selected by the mind and are not in the mind. Knowing, in other words, involves a peculiar transcendence. Critical realism parted company with both idealism and pragmatism by holding the belief in a known transcendent object. It parted with neo-realism by maintaining that knowing is not a relationship but an activity. Instead of the object being literally given to the mental acts of knowing, it is selected and interpreted in terms of conceptions. The thing is external to the act and independent of it. Our consciousness in perceiving expresses the *intention* of the mind built into and around organic response. The transcendence is referential and not literal.

Knowing is an act and knowledge an achievement which the act claims to contribute. "It is for this reason," states Sellars, "that I speak of all acts of cognition as cognitive claims."[24]

Note that he now says in the sixth principle that knowing involves "a peculiar transcendence," whereas in 1908 he had written that the "transcendence of experience is a pseudo-problem." Are these contentions contradictory? The answer involves the difference between "knowing" and "experience." We do not, Sellars claimed in 1929, actually experience things. We refer to and characterize things. Sellars equated experience with the direct awareness of subjective states and components. Sense data are experienced. Their referral to things is a going beyond experience per se. "I should like at this stage to point out," he wrote, "that the critical realist much prefers to use the term knowing rather than the term experiencing wherever he has to do with definite acts of cognition. Experiencing seems to cover both what Professor Alexander calls enjoying and what he calls contemplation. Thus a criticism such as that passed on critical realism by Professor Macintosh seems to the critical realist question-begging. Knowing the external world seems to him to depend on experiencing it, and yet it is clear that, for him, experiencing is a kind of knowing . . .: 'In other words, if we can experience the physical we can test our ideas of it and know it; if we can never experience it, it does not seem that we can have knowledge of it.' "[25] "Here," continued Sellars, "experiencing would seem to be a kind of immediate giveness of the object . . . I do not deny that this is the sort of thing that naïve realism encourages us to believe in. I simply assert that reflection makes us unable to retain the outlook and leads us to develop certain vital distinctions. . . . I hold that perception is a knowing of an elementary sort but that this knowing (cognitional giveness) is easily confused with the existential giveness of the object known. . . . Knowing is never a literal giveness of the object in the private stream of consciousness. An object given to the mind is not given in the mind."[26] We do not intuit physical things.

In the interests of the individuality of conscious experience — and to avoid the panpsychist problem of experience in general — Sellars conceived experience to be purely subjective. This sealed-envelope conception of experience is Sellars' official theory. At the same time, he used the term from time to time in a broader sense as in talking about the full-orbed "perceptual experience." In *Evolutionary Naturalism,* (1922) for example, Sellars writes that experience indicates an actual causally-based correlation between the physical existent and the datum. In 1939, again, he states that the "perceptual experience includes the category of thinghood, and with it denotation and characterization."[27] In "Sensations as Guides to Perceiving" in 1959 he asserts that "any knower has to start from his perceptual experience and its referential claims . . ."[28] Professor Sellars thus has ingredients for an open-ended view of individual experience — with its objective referrals, actions on things, undergoings, and evaluations. There is a tension, however, in some of his writing, between his official view of experience and his larger perspective.

The point of importance for us, nonetheless, is that insofar as experience is conceived in subjective terms, perceptual knowing goes beyond it in denoting and characterizing things that thereby become objects. There is an outreach of the organism to specific entities distinguished as such. Ostensible epistemological dualism, accordingly, passes into a functional epistemological monism; so much so, in fact, that Sellars is able to say in 1932 that "if the expression epistemological dualism stands for anything more than the recognition of the mechanism of perception, I reject it."[29] In 1939, Sellars made a still stronger statement: "Critical realism has nothing to do with dualism of any variety."[30]

There is a succinctness, however, about Sellars' later writing on referential realism that does not appear in his *Philosophy of Physical Realism.* This stands out, first, in his 1949 chapter on "Materialism and Human Knowing," and marks a further stage in the development of his epistemological position.[31] This stage culminates in a series of articles in 1959-63: "Sensations as Guides to Perceiving" (1959); "Levels of Causality . . ." (1959); "Referential Transcendence" (1961); "American Critical Realism and British Theories of Sense Perception" (1962); and "Direct Referential Realism" (1963).

That Sellars recognized these stages in his thinking is evidenced (1) by his repudiation of epistemological dualism in 1932, and (2) by his statement in 1969 regarding his 1930 philosophical credo.[32] In *Reflections on American Philosophy from Within* (1969), Sellars states:

> I can see how I was approaching my present analysis but had not yet quite clarified it. I spoke of reference and knowledge claims and looking through sensory data at the object. But I do not think that I had quite grasped how we use sensations to decipher facts about their controls. I spoke of logical characters in the content of perception. I would put it differently now. In the context of perceiving, we concentrate on features of sensory appearings as significant for the object we are perceiving. Accordingly, we begin to think the object in these terms.[33]

It was not only in succinctness, however, that the third stage points up Sellars' theory of perception. It is in its greater completeness and repleteness, with some reformulation. In treating "American Realism 1900-1930" for a Monist symposium,[34] I recall reading back into Sellars' 1932 principles his 1959-63 clarifications. His later findings are not therefore repudiations of his middle span but a sharpening and an amplifying of the basic position he has maintained throughout with its referential and logistical components.

"Materialism and Human Knowing" begins this sharpening and filling in, with the role of alertness, expectation, and bodily orientation as part of the dynamics of perceiving. These give a vectorial character to the process and set the stage for responses to certain types of stimuli under certain circumstances. Organic self-perception also enters and helps to give body to the environment; physical entities are coordinate with one's body. Perceiving and physical doing are thus connected, along with the employment of such categories as thinghood, endurance, causality, space-time — all blending together in a context of dynamic substantialism.

Cognition is a unique process. Its only approximations are those instinctive modes of patterned behavior below the level of conscious problem-solving; and though those approximations may seem close, they are not readily adjustable.

The tests of cognition take the forms of coherence, responsibility to data, prediction, and pragmatic control. Contra the constructionism of either Dewey or Russell, cognition is objective in import from the beginning. In knowing, we get facts or truths about the structure, composition, and behavior of things. But we must literally use our heads; the heart of critical realism is mentation or reflective activity. Mentation is selective and integrative. It pinpoints its data and issues. Reasoning as such is an operation resting on a capacity to bring together diverse data. It is a high-level type of causal process with rational effects.

What is achieved at this part of stage three is a measure of incisiveness. What is still left out is the fact and import of input and output, highly significant for gaining and developing relevant concepts. Sellars, we have noted, had early written on the functional development of the categories, and he had in the 1920's recognized the role of the from-and-to circuit in perceiving, but the force of these acknowledgments had to wait on information and communication theories for their adequate appreciation. He had not adequately recognized until the 1950's the role of feedback in the building of conceptions and the clarifying of perceptions. His position became notably more incisive with this insertion.

One example which he used to show the relation of output to input is that of throwing at a target, when we use our observation of our misses to correct our throws. An even clearer instance is that of shooting at a target where one can compensate quite deliberately for the deviations from the center.

Similarly in knowing one early learns to distinguish mushrooms from toadstools and varieties of mushrooms from each other, as well as good eggs from bad, etc., etc. As George Pitcher finds in experimental studies of perceiving, feedback in terms of information of successes and failures is effective in inducing better comprehensions, if rewards and punishments are not otherwise provided.[35] With such feedback, perceiving can become highly accurate and sophisticated.

We can now therefore fill in the "picture" of the components of the process of perceptual knowing. Perceiving is no mere having of sensations; sensations are not terminal. Nor is perceiving the mere registering of the givenness of objects. The process is more involved and is built around the interaction of an organism and its surroundings: the operation of stimuli from entities in the environing world; the arising of sensory qualities as evidential of things in that world; the response of the organism to the thing (be it the moon in the "heavens," the snake in the grass, the fruit on the tree, or the tree in the path); the feedback from the initial response (and from later responses) in terms of burns, bites or injuries, on one side, and satisfactions or gratifications on the other; the formation of concepts which characterize things and distinguish types of things and types of situations from each other and provide the differentiation for individual things from each other. Perception without conception, as Kant said, is blind; and conception without perception is empty. Hence the importance of perception for meaningful thought and the importance of conception for discrimination *per se*.

The core of the process of perceiving is the direct discriminating referral to substantial entities coupled with their characterization and resultant knowing. Perception is no less direct though mediated nor is it less a case of knowing because it is an involved achievement. It is a dynamic achievement in which the organism reaches out to other things: to appropriate, assimilate, utilize, ward off, escape from, enjoy, and, finally, to understand.

Levels of Knowing

Perceptual knowledge, Sellars states, is "an elementary . . . kind of knowing."[36] Yet how rudimentary it is depends on the conceptual framework that enters into it. There are diverse levels of perception. Sellars distinguishes quick perception from more sophisticated kinds. There is a big difference between the perception of a fruit, such as an apple or an orange, and the perception of the moon; and there have been wide differences in the perception of the moon.

Perceptual knowledge, at whatever level, has a complex matrix. In its most rudimentary form, it rests on neuromuscular mechanisms; neuromuscular patterns are the basis for conscious discriminations. Sellars refers to the operation of these patterns on an instinctive level as a sort of implicit knowing, yet gives as an example the learned habits of the skilled tennis player. A still clearer instance, I think, would be the coordinations of Olympic pairs-skaters who have built their knowledge and reflections into synchronized activities. In such examples, knowledge which had been explicit has become implicit. Its neuro-muscular basis is, of course, quite evident. With the acknowledgment of the "from-and-to circuit" as the core of perceptual knowing, the neurophysiology of perceiving is a corollary. "It is a truism in biology and physiology," states Sellars, "that organic activities connected with external adjustment are directional and patterned. . . . There is a capacity for integrated activity of remarkable complexity." This is the organic matrix of knowledge.

"It is because the nervous system is pattern-reproducing that there can be discrimination and delicacy of adjustment."[37] Felt awareness is born in organic attention. Conceptual patterns develop on this same neuro-physiological base.

Scientific knowing is on a quite different level from typical perceptual knowing, though it starts from and comes back to the latter. One evident difference indeed lies in the microscopic (and macroscopic) perspectives and analyses of science. But there is also a different symbolization in science. Pictorial language is imprecise. Hence science comes to use the language of mathematics (and mathematical logic). Experimentation, the commonly assumed earmark of science, takes on its special character in science because of the development of system and precision. Scientific knowing, therefore, is the product of a much more complicated technique. New data are discovered and new concepts are formulated because of the use of instruments, inclusive of mathematics, and because of the development of hypotheses that direct research. The achievement of hypothetico-deductive methods lifts science to a quite different level from that of mere perception, though these methods also refer to the perceived world and start out from the perceived world.

The common denominators between scientific and perceptual knowing are worth noting. Both aim at knowledge of external things. The interpretation of data is characteristic of each; the pull is from the data but toward their meanings. Reflection enters into all but the most rudimentary cases of either.

Reason has historically been placed in opposition to sensing, but it is not just the kind of thing it appears to be in pure mathematics. We cannot justifiably think of it as a faculty of an intuitive and absolute sort. The goal of knowing is disclosure, and reasoning stands for all those methods and operations that help in the solution of problems: the developing of technique; the development and application of inductive canons; the employment of creative imagination. "In short, reason is a term which covers the way the mind works in systematic investigation," declares Sellars.[38] Reason is an *integral factor* in science, and is common in perceptual experience.

What happens in science is a gradual transformation and deepening of the categories of thought. New predicates are developed, such as energy, gravitation, time as measurement, elasticity, mass. Science adds to the organic mechanisms, methods of perception, invented instruments, techniques, and system. Hence we have in science a combination of aided and extended perception, technique of measurement and experimentation, application of mathematics, theoretical construction, hypothetico-deductive method, and consequent reformulation of the categories. Yet science makes observations and draws inferences which presuppose the framework of perceptual knowledge. And insofar as science deals in content rather than the formalities of logic and mathematics, it is ontological in interests and objectives. In spite of all the "isms" in the philosophy of science (positivism, operationalism, conventionalism, Kantianism, etc.), empirical science is substantialistic in its primary concerns.

The Philosophical Level of Knowing

In view of Sellars' deep regard for science it is not surprising that he conceived philosophy as an interpretation of existence and of perennial problems (the mind-body problem for example) in *close relationship with science.* Science is the most precise and best informed species of human activity within its own compass. Philosophy needs the findings and other materials of science. But philosophy has its own concerns and perspectives and these go beyond those of science.

In his treatment of levels of knowing in 1932, Sellars did not distinguish a philosophical level as such; but he has always held that there was philosophical knowing and that philosophy goes beyond science in two important respects: first, in investigating the assumptions of science — in his case, investigating the main concepts and categories of science. "Science," he wrote, "requires a philosophical completion, not as regards facts and theories, but with respect to its categorial setting."[39] After studying Ernst Mach, Karl Pearson, and James Ward extensively, Sellars — as we have already shown — wrote extensively on the categories. Here was a philosophical issue worthy of the best minds, as Kant and Hegel illustrated, but neither of the latter had a biological perspective. And the categories need to be approached via their evolution as biological functions. They need to be viewed, first of all, in their role in perceptual knowledge and then in their functions in conceptual structures or systems.

The philosophy of the categories, in other words, is part of the theory of knowledge, i.e., the theory of knowing about knowing not just in the psychological sense but in the larger integrative sense which encompasses biology, physiology, neurology, psychology in a number of its interests, logic, information theory, philosophy of language, etc.

But this brings us to the second sense in which philosophy goes beyond science: its integration of findings from all relevant sciences for the solution of basic problems. The mind-body relation and the problem of perceptual knowledge are two of these fundamental questions on which Sellars himself utilized the findings of a range of sciences. We have already discussed the development of his theory of perceptual knowledge: the contributions of behavioral studies, i.e., of stimulus response psychology (gestaltist as well as behaviorist), the inputs and outputs of information and communication theories, the biological functions evolutionarily conceived. Philosophy, of course, wrote Sellars, "works with the sciences, physical, biological, social. It has . . . its own momentum and perspective to keep in mind, that is, a combination of interaction and parallelism,"[40] with the sciences. This relationship will be more fully demonstrated later in treating the mind-body problem.

We shall also, in the next chapter, treat philosophical knowing of ontological referents and, in a later chapter, knowing with regard to human values. Not that philosophical thought is to be defined solely or perhaps even largely as a species of knowing; but there is a distinctive ingredient of knowledge in a balanced or penetrating philosophical perspective: a knowledge of a different set of relationships than those we find in any of the sciences. Philosophical perspectives are informative of relations that are otherwise ignored; and in the field of human values and their relationship to activities and procedures, these can be of paramount importance. "A Cosmic view and a planetary view, a social view and an intrinsically personal view: these must be woven into a well-evidenced and constantly tested perspective," concludes Sellars.[41]

CHAPTER 3

Substantive Emergent Naturalism

IT IS difficult to date the beginning of Sellars' emergent naturalism. His volume on *Evolutionary Naturalism* was published in 1922, the year Lloyd Morgan gave his Gifford Lectures on Emergent Evolution, and Samuel Alexander published his essay on "Natural Piety." But five of Sellars' chapters were published well in advance of his book, and one of them, "A Thing and Its Properties," antedated the book by seven years. Other chapters — on Space, Time, and Causality, respectively — are anticipated by writings that date back to 1908 and 1909; while his *Critical Realism*, completed in 1913 although not published until 1916, suggests a companion volume to come on metaphysics.[1] It is not surprising, therefore, that Sellars should recount that in 1909 he "was bold enough to outline" for Bergson "the idea of emergence in contrast to his more vitalistic stance."[2] Sellars' naturalism indeed seems to have come with his mother's milk and his father's medical biology; his emergent evolutionism, with his reflections on twentieth-century science and its import for a theory of evolution. Lloyd Morgan, Sellars reports, indeed, thought that Sellars was probably the first public expositor of emergent evolution.

One point is evident: Sellars' evolutionary naturalism was a growth over a significant number of years, beginning at least as early as 1908 and extending into the 1940's. We shall attempt first to trace the continuity of his thought from 1908 to 1922.

I

In two articles in 1908,[3] Sellars presents reality as a process, stereometric and therefore structured, yet in the nature of the case undergoing structural change. "Process," he says, "portrays to my mind the dynamic character of reality. It signifies that 'to be' is 'to be active.' By working from this category we can avoid the problem of substratum . . . or identity which somehow possesses change, or of which change is an adjective. . . . A chemical reaction is no longer regarded as a mere exchange of partners, but as a complex process of establishing equilibrium in a disturbed system of energies. Rest is, also, explained by motion, not motion by rest. A complete reversal is thus made from the static view of permanence to the dynamic view of process."[4] Sellars himself was never addicted to the static view of matter; hence the smooth development to an emergent evolutionism.

Sellars continues his 1908 exposition: "But how can the demand for stability and continuance be satisfied in this apparent Heracliteanism? In two ways: first, conservation is an experimental fact, which unlike permanence, does not exclude change, but implies it. Second, organization supplies a relatively permanent structure to reality."[5]

But organization is not to be conceived in Aristotelian terms as a kind of joining of form and an abstract matter. Organization may indeed be analyzed into structure and function, but function is the natural dynamics of structure. Let us suppose that "reality as a process organizes itself in various ways, and that we through experimentation and reflection, can comprehend the organization on both the structural and functional sides, this comprehension, on our part, does not imply that the organization is an entity residing in various things."[6] Organization is the very pattern of process.

If, accordingly, we "conceive reality as a stereometrical process more complicated in some portions than in others . . . yet constantly in the moving stress of the reciprocal adaptation and self-achievement of its parts, we can gain the idea of an immanent change in no wise opposed to the conservation of energies or capacities. . . . Change is a comparative term, and to call the universe a process does not imply that the organizations or 'forms' of its parts vary in monotonous uniformity. A process is capable of differential organization — this is the essential significance of evolution — and these forms may have all degrees of stability from that of the so-called atom to the shifting variancy of the higher cortical areas."[7]

The upshot of the fact of differential organization is the emergence of different types and levels of causal systems. Causality has been misconceived throughout human history. Aristotle's four types of cause were abstractions from the actual causal situation; similarly, the later rationalist identification of cause with reason. "As is well known the cause was for a long time identified with the 'ground' or sufficient reason. Hume it was who brought into general recognition its temporal and empirical as against its rational character. . . . As I have defended the reality of time as change, it is evident that I must regard as erroneous the identification of cause with the reason or the explanation."[8] Similarly Hume's sequential analysis of cause is purely subjective. Ontologically, we must keep "clearly in mind the fact of a continuous change in some system . . ." Causality is an immanent process within a specific system. Organization must be regarded as "essential to the nature of any causal process."[9]

The "complexity of organization," moreover, "may well have increased in parts of reality." The evolutionary findings and outlook of science support this. Hence, the arising of different types of causal system. An organism and its environment form a special type of causal system. This result gives a "*doctrine of grades of causal relation and activity dependent on the organization* of the interacting parts of a . . . system. With this view granted, the qualitative at last received recognition, and the real presence of variety, on which evolution depends, is faced."[10]

"What other agent to account for direct change is thinkable?" Structural evolutionary change "has at least three merits: first, that of accounting for the conservation of past activity; second, that of furnishing a pivot for development; third, the merit of control. Only when these three aspects are understood in their interrelation can evolution be grasped."[11]

An example of cumulative complexity is found in psychology. "Habits are the precipitate of activity, they are the means for the development of new habits and they also control the kind of habits to be formed at least in part."[12] "The type of causal process depends on the organization of the interacting nodes of reality. . . . Man of course with his tremendously delicate and functional organization presents the highest type of causal reaction, ordinarily called teleological."[13] This type of causality Sellars later designates as agential: the causality of conscious choice and control. The individual may choose and act in terms of his own nature. The choice is then determined by the system, but the system allows for the entertaining and calculating of alternative courses of action. This is the sort of behavior commonly regarded as free, but is no less caused by the components of the system, issuing in the decisions and purposeful actions of the individual. This level of causality is quite different from that of inorganic mechanics. The system is much more complicated, and the activity of the brain in calculating values and directing action is a particularly important additional factor. We have here an emergent development, and emergent evolution is thus present in the 1908-1909 papers.

Sellars' *Critical Realism* (1916) is preeminently epistemological. He leaves basic cosmological and ontological questions to a later volume. But there are advances or at least clarifications in the *Critical Realism* pointing to a distinctively emergent naturalism. On page 233, for example, he contrasts his position with that of William James. James asserts in his *Principles of Psychology* that if evolution is to work smoothly, consciousness of some shape must have been present at the very origin of things.[14] "This statement," writes Sellars, "arises out of his belief that the brain is nothing but the self-same atoms which make the nebula, jambed and temporarily caught in peculiar positions. For this view the relations between the atoms are external, and organizations which are more than arrangements do not exist for nature. I, on the contrary, take evolution to mean the development of wholes which are not merely collections of units."[15]

"All depends on the nature of the system within which intelligence is at work, whether or not it is limited to the connection of sames within a series." The principle of continuity must not be taken in such a way as to exclude the emergence of novelties. "A true empiricism . . . recognizes that newness occurs in nature as it does in our experience,"[16] and the question is an open one regarding the conditions under which newness occurs. "The assertion," for example, "that matter is conscious under certain circumstances does not, because consciousness is unextended, conflict with the assertion that matter is extended."[17] The question is whether consciousness is to be conceived as a substance or a variant, and if the latter, what it is a variant or function of.

Since reality is process, evolution surely implies change in the mode of activity of the parts of nature. Nature is not a dead level system. It develops grades of causal activity in its evolving. The kinds of activity characteristic of brains within organisms ought, therefore, to be notably different from that of rocks or trees. the capacities for conscious endeavors may well be, and indeed evidently are, a unique feature of cerebral processes as such.

We are thus rather clearly on our way to a full theory of emergent evolution. The "physical world rises to the level of purposive activity, and . . . consciousness is an immanently produced variant in such a physical world."[18] *Evolutionary Naturalism*, the 1922 publication, is essentially the rounding out of the theory.

It starts with a statement of the requirements of an adequate naturalism. The one inclusive requirement is that it shall provide adequately for everything distinguishably human as part of nature. Man is "a very complex whole, immersed and functioning in nature" but is he actually as a whole person a part of nature? Two basic conditions to be met are: (1) an adequate naturalism must "demonstrate the validity of physical realism as an epistemology"; (2) it must "point out the possibility of reconciling determinism with empirical freedom."[19] It must also, of course, naturalize human values, including those of religion. We shall treat these further tasks of naturalism in the last three chapters. The problems of a naturalistic epistemology and of a naturalistic account of human agency are the basic matters to be accounted for here. Having already dealt with epistemology in Chapter 2, a relevant summation is all that is needed. But what, first, is the nature of emergent naturalism?

It is an outright evolutionary cosmology, contra those views which would separate mind, soul, or reason from the evolving existents. Evolution is a complex process of cumulative change producing new wholes that rise on "the intimate combination of recoverable, yet for the time changed, parts."[20] It is not qualities per se (as Samuel Alexander maintained) that emerge, but new wholes or unities with notable capacities or properties. Capacities, activities, and organizations have grown step by step on preceding changes. New potentialities go with such factors as new organization and cumulative powers. The admission by scientists of creative synthesis in nature has also brought the recognition of "critical points" at which new properties emerge.[21] We are thus confronted with novel additions accruing in nature. Though Sellars does not use the word "accrue," it seems especially appropriate to his theory of genetic continuity as cumulative older properties are transcended yet included.

Emergent evolution therefore contains two elements that are equally real: genetic continuity and novelty. The former indeed is modified by the latter so that the continuity is genetic and not purely logical, i.e., it is developmental. The emergence of the novel in nature thus means that creativity can and does occur in nature and we do not need to have recourse to a special super-physical agency.

The organism is a striking case of creatively cumulative integration: "A richer and more empirical approach to biology has

[thus] opened before us."[22] "It is the thesis of evolutionary naturalism that the organism includes consciousness and is the sole source of that differential behavior which distinguishes it."[23]

The organism is more than the sum of its parts. It is an organization in which the whole exerts control over the parts. This controlled behavior of the parts is thereby an example of a level of causality in nature that is expressive of organization or creative synthesis. It is the *organization* of existents which is basically novel and with which new properties are correlated. In sum therefore we can say that:

1) Organization is objectively significant and causally effective.

2) Function and structure go together; function is the active side or phase of structure.

3) Evolution is the active rise of new wholes with new properties, the higher level resting on but carrying out the potentialities of the lower.[24]

We can now come back to our queries concerning (1) the adequacy of the epistemology of evolutionary naturalism, and (2) the possibility that it might reconcile determinism with empirical freedom. We have in Chapter 2 already traced the epistemology through three stages and have found that it is no passive receiving of percepts but a complex, active process concerned, in the first instance, with the survival and growth of the organism. We must also recall that though Sellars thought of himself as an epistemological dualist at the time of the publication of his *Evolutionary Naturalism*, the two basic strands of his theory were (1) its natural, active referentialism, and (2) its functional categorizing of entities in their circumstances. Sellars' later theory dispenses with the epistemological dualism by distinguishing between the mechanism of knowing and the achievement of knowing objects as such; and it fills out the process with its quales as clues and cues, its response to the sources of the stimulation, the feedback from the responses, consequent conceptualizings of the objects, and more adequate discrimination. All of this is a biologically based natural process giving functional knowledge of external things yet setting the groundwork for disinterested inquiry. There is a clear continuity between normal perceiving and scientific knowing despite the big differences in the content of their respective sophistications. Science itself indeed, as well as ordinary perception, can be shown to be most intelligible in the light of evolutionary naturalism. And Sellars' analyses of the main concepts of science were governed by this maxim.

There remains then the problem of reconciling determinism with empirical freedom. This again is an issue on which Sellars wrote a number of essays. While each essay arises out of a different set of circumstances and was directed to a different type of situation, there is no evidence of a basic change of position from his first essay on "Causality" (1909) to his "Guided Causality, Using Reason and 'Free Will' " (1959)[25] or his "Agential Causality."[26] There is simply an extensive elaboration or filling out. Sellars himself refers repeatedly to his 1909 article with its distinction of grades of causality. He was soon to substitute the term "levels " for "grades" of causality, and this theme is probably dealt with most adequately in a 1959 article on "Levels of Causality: The Emergence of Guidance and Reason in Nature."[27] The theme of this essay is the enlargement of the category of efficient causality to provide for a special kind of immanent causality: the causality of agency. Our treatment of this theme must here be skeletal and merely suggestive. There is no attempt, first of all, to deny or denounce determinism or to make some provision for indeterminism, though there is a recognition of empirical indeterminacy, i.e., problems to be resolved, with alternatives to be chosen.

Causality in the organic sphere indeed has different levels. It appears in a more rudimentary sense in the form of guided response: "A diving bird, like the gannet, behaves somewhat like a guided missile. The usual apparatus is linked to established muscular patterns. Learning is largely an affair of maturing and adjusting. What happens in man, differentially, is that his foundational framework is developed and lifted to a higher *causal level* by means of new cortical abilities. Complex skills are learned and this know-how is integral to concept formation and *knowing that*" such and such is the case.[28]

The causal mode of conceptual reasoning is a different level from that of elemental guided response. "Thought has its roots in the need to modify and direct impulse just as it has other roots in the need to direct perceiving. Neither impulse nor perceiving could serve the human organism adequately without the insertion of thought or intelligence."[29] There is a discovery of the basic importance of evidence and consistency; also the need to perceive clearly and to think adequately. What we must formally correlate, however, are powers, methods, guiding criteria, and ends. This correlation issues in what has historically been called the human will.

The will is the power of the agential self, responsible to itself for the appropriate treatment of the things in its neighborhood. The reputed freedom of the will is a clear case of immanent causality with projective teleology, i.e., governed by human purposes and needs. All this will become much clearer when we have completed our study of Sellars' emergent naturalism and dealt with his treatment of the mind-brain problem. We hope, meantime, that this preliminary statement is sufficiently directional to serve our immediate purpose.

II

The story of Sellars' emergent naturalism is now half told. The second half involves a new caption: *Reformed Materialism*. As late as 1927 Sellars wrote an essay in defense of a naturalism which was not just a materialism.[30] Historically, materialism had not met the requirements of an adequate naturalism, by integrating what is distinctive of man into nature. Its epiphenomenalisms did not allow for effective consciousness, actual values, or even certified knowledge. But naturalism with an adequate recognition of the role of the physical could do this.

When, however, Sellars found the term "naturalism" sweepingly preempted for a methodology — the methodology of the sciences — without recognition of the basic importance of ontology,[31] he promptly decided that the time had come for a physicalist ontology clearly designated as such. His had been a substantive physical naturalism from the start. His emergent naturalism had centered in the synthetic process by which new substances came into being. Might not this process disclose the real nature of a material universe? Why should the term materialism be limited to its inadequate forms: Democritean, Hobbesian, Marxist? How else indeed conceive a world of physical systems, whatever their level of causality, than as a material world? The time had therefore come for an updated, and hence reformed, materialism which would do justice to all the possibilities in physical systems.

A series of essays in the forties elaborated this possibility. They include: Causality and Substance" (1943), "Is Naturalism Enough?" (1944), "Does Naturalism Need Ontology?" (1944), "Reformed Materialism and Intrinsic Endurance" (1944), "Can a Reformed Materialism do Justice to Values?" (1944), "Reflections on Dialectical Materialism" (1944), "Materialism and Relativity" (1946), "Materialism and Human Knowing" (1949).

The case against physical substance had not been adequately made. It rested on a faulty epistemology (which simplistically held that we can only experience elements of experience) and on an equally faulty ontology (which conceived of substance as an amorphous matrix or substrate in which qualities inhered — like quills in a porcupine). In each case there was a neglected alternative: that experiences were guides to physical responses, hence open-ended, and that organization and activity were intrinsic to physical systems. Causality is a characteristic or literal function of physical systems. And causality involves a whole set of connected categories. Space, time, activity, tendency, potentiality and emergence are some of these. But the superordinate category involved in causality is that of substance. The setting of causality is thus ontological.[32]

By linking causality with substance taken in a dynamic sense we are able to distinguish three kinds of causality: (1) transeunt causality as in the action of one thing on another in any mechanical relation (the bat on the ball, for example); (2) immanent causality which is activity within a system, as in the case of activity bestirred by an extra flow of adrenalin consequent on an exciting thought. How such a physical system arises in the first place we have accounted as an emergent development. (3) Emergent causality is a special kind in its very own right. Emergent causality is a synthetic causality due to the coming together of a special set of factors under precise conditions. We shall illustrate this soon with the Stanley Miller and Sidney Fox experiments.

The drama of emergent evolution is not indicated by the foregoing discussion. The vast divide between primal inorganic existence and agential entities such as ourselves has been thought by many to require creative imagination and creative fiat. But the terrific wastefulness of nature's experiments is not accounted for on such a basis. Nor is the origin of such a creative genius. The hypothesis in fact more than begs the question. As a post-Darwinian, certainly, Sellars had more to work with than his predecessors. But he did not have this problem solved for him.

How does life itself arise, whatever its type or form? This is a basic question, and it is a different question from that of the origin of any certain species. Darwin saw the issue involved and the kind of experiment that might be crucial. But he did not have the solution, and creative evolutionists, as we have intimated, only accented the mystery.

The thesis of Sellars' emergent evolution, however, is that new entities which are not at all predictable emerge under very special conditions. Life — or, rather *living things are just such emergents.* In a recent edition of his *Principles and Problems of Philosophy* published under a modified title,[33] Sellars gives a dramatic description of these processes of emergence. In his chapter "The Nature and Origin of Life," Sellars argues for a recognition of an 'involution' in nature, that is, for the emergence of a technique of awareness that supplements and indeed enlarges nature. Refractions and reflections of light are, in fact, translated into the colors of the rainbow and the sunset.

But before techniques of awareness could begin there had to be rudiments of life; and before any mode of life, chemical evolution was prerequisite. Sellars quotes Darwin as follows: "But if . . . we could conceive . . . that in some little pond, with all sorts of ammonia and phosphoric salts, light, heat, electricity, etc. present, a protein compound was chemically formed, ready to undergo still more changes . . ."[34] there might be the possibility of all kinds of life. But there had to be the pond and the salts, electricity, etc., and the conditions of valence.

"I have, quite naturally, been impressed by the electronic interpretation of valence," wrote Sellars in the original manuscript of *Principles, Perspectives, and Problems of Philosophy*, "and the way in which the properties of chemical substances, that is, the way they behave, can be explained by molecular structure. Hydrogen bonding has turned out to be very important. There is great variety here. . . . Water is an important type of molecule for life . . . no other liquid is as suitable for the support of life. . . . It acts readily as a solvent and has a high latent heat of evaporation. . . .

"Oxygen is another molecule with remarkable properties; it is highly reactive. Because of this, the primitive atmosphere contained little of it. Early forms of life had to make use of carbon dioxide. But in producing oxygen, they make possible more efficient chemical processes."[35]

"A good paleontologist, Gaylord Simpson, is amazed by the story of evolution. It is as unlikely as is a [specific] hand of cards . . . He doubts that hominids could have arisen on other planets."[36]

And, coming back to molecules, "these have replaced appeals to slime-like protoplasm and to colloids. . . . Nucleic acids [most notably] were a puzzle when they were first discovered. Now DNA, deoxyribose nucleic acid, is regarded as constituting the herditary substance of the chromosomes. Its structure, as worked out by Watson and Crick, was in terms of a double helix. It is terribly large and complex and composed of [many] units. These . . . in union with phosphorus, make up the nucleotides. The result is giant molecules. In the thirties no one knew what to make of nucleic acids . . . One now thinks of DNA as a chain having a molecular weight of at least 100,000,000 . . . The average molecular weight of a nucleotide is about 300, so there would be over 300,000 nucleotides (in an DNA chain).

"RNA is another form of nucleic acid which differs in the sugar portion of the molecule. It is believed to have different functions in translating the genes into the protein enzymes they determine. (One speaks of [i.e., distinguishes] messenger RNA and transfer RNA.)"[37]

These are extremely complex chemical devices. "It must have taken a very long time for their emergence. . . . The essentials of this are supposed to have occured before biological evolution as we now know it."[38] But how did biological evolution get started? Life comes from cells, and these from previous cells. But how did cells themselves come to be?

Darwin's idea of a warm little pond, with ammonia, phosphorus, electricity, etc., afforded chemical evolutionists with clues. According to Sellars: "The guiding idea was to reproduce as nearly as possible the atmosphere and energy conditions of the earth in its early days. It had then what is called a 'reducing' atmosphere. There was very little oxygen present. That seems to have come with photosynthesis in its various stages."[39]

In 1953 Dr. Stanley Miller made the classic experiment. Working under the direction of Noble Laureate Harold Urey, he sent 60,000 volts of electricity through a series of condensers, flasks, and tubing containing nothing but ammonia, methane, hydrogen and water. Gradually the water in the boiling flask became darker. On careful analysis, Miller found that the water now contained many organic substances, including amino acids, the building blocks of protein. Sellars notes that "Dr. Sidney Fox . . . has carried on investigations similar to Miller's. It is surprising what complex molecules were found."[40]

Crucial points in this process, Sellars points out, are:

1) The emergence of interconnections giving the forms within which chemical processes occurred. One of these patterns was genic.

2) Specific advances toward archebiosis, including the development of water and carbon and the earth's overall fitness for life. "No mention is now made of protoplasm, for the theory has now shifted to molecular integrations. Life in the strict sense, was prepared for and flowered *as oxygen became more abundant.*[41]

3) Organisms which were "most viable in their niches had a preponderance of survivors and so affected the gene pool for their species."[42] (Certain mutations may be thus both better suited to the conditions of existence and also, in the case of 'higher' organisms, more adaptable. These, in turn, modify the gene pool.) There was, in this way, a directionality without conscious purpose, and yet the possibility for the emergence of the whole conscious, reflectively experimental, and enjoying life of man. Specialization of tissues, indeed, opens the way to that tremendously complex yet marvelously concentrated natural computer, man's brain, and to coordinate systems of glands and organs that develop over vast eras. Sensitivity enlarges into clearly referential feelings and conscious discrimination. These function in conjuction with behavior as natural developments toward the guidance of organisms by sensations. And this, in turn, is fundamental to the development of signs, symbols, images, and "earmarks" and their uses in ratiocination as well as in organic adjustment. Self-direction, control from within or agential causality, is thus organically developed. Experimental inventiveness, which emerges from trial and error, and reflective processes explicitly appear. Nature thus rises to conscious creativity but not apart from man. There are numerous philosophers indeed who want the mind to stand, metaphorically of course, on its own feet. The hemispheres of the brain (in the body) *are* the mind's feet.

In his earlier writing, we have noted, going back to 1909, Sellars had distinguished levels of causality in nature. These, in due course he discovers, are of three clear types (1) transeunt causality (from the Latin *transeo*) as when one is propelled forward by an impact from behind; (2) immanent causality as when a secretion affects the digestion or alertness of an individual; and (3) emergent causality as in the arising of a new substance from a new synthesis of elements or factors. Agential causality is a special form of immanent causality. It involves a high level of discrimination, with a distinctive capacity for entertaining and evaluating possibilities, to function on the level of agential causality. But it is causality within a physical system. Sellars has thus shown something of the great range of possibilities in physical systems.

The basic importance of substance stands out in this evolutionary drama. As Sellars states in "Causality and Substance," (1943), "I take substance to be a category to whose full conception all our knowledge of self and things is necessary."[43] All existence is in the form of substances. Substance is a term for a physical system, an entity, a denotable. But substances disintegrate as well as integrate. What then is the ultimate stuff of reality? What has intrinsic endurance?

Sellars addressed an expecially important essay to this question in 1943, "Reformed Materialism and Intrinsic Endurance."[44] It was this essay that was the occasion of DeWitt Parker's statement that "No American has done more persistent and original thinking on the fundamental philosophical problems in the last thirty years or so than my colleague, Professor Sellars."[45] This essay might be labeled R. W. Sellars' metaphysics, since it concerns the question, What is there, if anything, beyond or behind existence? What is it that actually endures? How is endurance possible?

There are two things that are said by different groups to endure eternally. One group holds that the only thing that persists is mind (a common argument of course is the unempirical one that mind or soul is simple and indecomposable). The second group, holding to the eternity of matter, is influenced by the law of conservation of material energy. This second group, too, has a very considerable history, going back not only to Leucippus and Democritus, but to their Ionian forerunners. Thus there have long been people who have held that the cosmos exists in its own right and is material in its basic nature. And thus they have denied the contingency of the world.

What is distinctive of modern, twentieth-century materialism is its integral dynamics. It is in their *becoming* that physical systems have intrisic endurance. "Matter," says Sellars, "I take to be active, dynamic, relational, and self-organizing." "It is likewise endurant, having an endurance which goes with activity. . . . All composite existents . . . are maintained by activity. My divergence from eventism [á la Whitehead, Dewey, et al] had roots other than a desire to defend outgrown notions of substance. Rather it is the expression of realism as against sensationalism [which attempts to build persisting entities out of sensations or hypotheses]. Those who build on sensations as Whitehead and Russell do, cannot accept substantiveness and force."[46]

A basic problem for materialism, we have noted, has been the problem of knowledge. Even Marxism, with a dynamic conception of matter, and later with Lenin's reflection theory of perceptual knowledge, advanced little beyond Lockian dualism.[47] Lenin was aware of the problem, however, and was trying to surmount the epistemological divide. We have seen Sellars' referentialism as a bridge from minds to things, a bridge rooted in the biological and psychological development of man. Reformed materialism, therefore, no longer has this problem.

But how conceive of matter so that it is at once expressed in distinct things that perish and is also eternally endurant; so that it is the type of thing on which the categories are founded (space, time, causality, process, pattern), yet a timeless stuff that can articulate itself in time? Sellars interestingly asserts that matter is always in the form of individual existents (denotables, particulars) and yet it is not, as in idealism, a principle of individuation. Matter is active, self-organizing and relational, but is not a kind of correlative potency as in Aristotle. Against Aristotelianism, reformed materialism emphasized a materialistic kind of hylomorphism in which matter itself involves both form and activity. Against Whitehead, reformed materialism united activity with intrinsic endurance and attributed both to matter. It further modified Aristotelian hylomorphism by substituting functional directionalism for formal finalism. It breaks likewise with classical mechanism and emphasizes intrinsic order and growth. Material existence must have the sort of being which is characterizable in terms of all the properties, forms, and relations of specific things and yet which survives their disappearance.

The term "stuff" of nature answers to this demand, though it is but another word for *being* taken relationally. It indicates the possibility of denotables which can be combined, separated, operated on, and can have a career of their own.

There has been too much neglect in post-Humean philosophy, of constants and constitution. We have a special example of a material system in the organic self. Here we have a privileged physical system,not only in that it is capable of conscious experience of qualitative characteristics, but privileged in the quite special sense of being on the inside, having both participative and external knowledge, and privileged in the sense of having knowledge directed at itself. It is the one clear case of being *für sich*. This is one type of substance in which we have knowledge of the *content of being:* sense qualities, feelings, images, memories, aspirations, struggles, etc. All other instances of knowledge are external: knowledge of the effects of one thing on another under diverse conditions, of standard relationships, etc.

An organic system therefore combines stuff, dynamic connections, conscious experience of all kinds, integrative and efficient causality and relative endurance. It is a quite special kind of substance.

The notion of substance is that of a dynamic organized whole. This is the modality of existence as such. There is a difference, however, between existence and being. The latter, *being*, is that which endures intrinsically and forever expresses itself in things which are generated, live their span, and vanish.

The highest emergent things we know are qualitative human organisms, distinguished, we have mentioned, by self-awareness. But self-awareness ceases at death. Yet the bodies remain for others to study. And scientists hold that the stuff of which they are composed is conserved. It is *this stuff which is being*, in contrast with the more specific modalities and individualities of existence.

Being is constantly expressing itself in composite denotables. Generation and corruption seem complementary. Activity and organization reside in the very essence of being. Matter implies process, and process implies matter. There are no absolute beginnings or endings. Generable qualities and capacities accompany being only implicitly. It is for this reason that the amount of being does not conflict with qualitative gain or loss. Quality is the changing *content of being* as integration proceeds and recedes.

Being is not directly denotable. We discover being in its processes and manifestations. The processes of being are, in turn, the producers of time. Time is the local relation of events to each other. It is thus ontological, involving as it does, the relation of things in process. We can, therefore, distinguish between real time and apparent time. Since, moreover, the stuff of being is intrinsically active, and generation and corruption are affairs of integration and disintegration, neither of them violating the principle of conservation which expresses the intrinsic endurance of being, eternity encompasses existential time or process — and is not something in opposition to it. Eternity accordingly is cumulative, yet always incomplete.

CHAPTER 4

The Minded Brain

THE crowning emergent of evolutionary process is the minded brain: a tremendously complex mechanism with all the capacities that being minded yields: to feel, to perceive, to recall, to imagine, to conceive, to think, to desire, to choose, to direct, to suffer, to enjoy, to resent, to hate, to love, to harmonize. How complex this organ is is seen in the contrast between a man's brain and that of a honeybee and yet how amazing is the brain of the bee. Sellars shows his admiration for its complexity in the following passage:

> The brain of the honey bee, we are told, weighs only a fraction of a gram and occupies a space smaller than a pinhead, yet it has the ability to produce and *interpret* complex signals and to profit by experience through learning. Each neuron of this tiny system is like a data-storing or data-processing module of an electronic brain. Yet the electronic brain requires a large space to carry out processes that are less complex than those carried out by this remarkable piece of equipment. Guidance systems in the honey bee are elaborate. The scout gives information by a series of rapid movements, bumping into other bees and communicating the scent of the nectar-bearing flowers. But this is not enough. Other bees must be informed of the distance and direction of the find. This language consists of waggling runs. Bee's eyes are sensitive to polarized light, and bee-dances vary with the quality of the food source. It is all very astonishing.[1]

"Birds constitute a second line of development," he continues. "As Herrick points out, the brain stem is enormously enlarged but the outlying cortex is reduced." But when you come to man's "big brain" you have a tremendously greater array of powers or capacities. The brain is minded in the fullest range of the meanings of *mind* and *consciousness*.

Appreciation of what this development means has had to wait for twentieth-century achievements in both cybernetics and psychology. The problem of the relationship of mind and body is a very old problem; yet it had to await Descartes' sharp discriminations to become fully acute. Later work, up to the twentieth century, saw philosophers on the sides of interactionist dualism, parallelism, idealistic psychic monism, and epiphenomenalist materialism. None of these views made an adequate case. Sellars found himself concerned with the problem from the very start in the light of evolution, new developments in science, behavioristic findings, and, later, cybernetics. He may be said indeed to have built his whole philosophy around the mind-body problem since, as James Ward said, its resolution was crucial for a naturalistic philosophy — and Sellars' orientation in both natural and social sciences disposed him toward naturalism.

He wrote four of his five earliest essays on this problem. In "The Nature of Experience" (1907),[2] he concerned himself with the individualistic character of experience, contra Dewey's view of experience in general and any panpsychist theory. In "Consciousness and Conservation" (1909),[3] he found the transiency of consciousness juxtaposed to the endurance of physical systems and posited consciousness as a variant of such a system. In "An Important Antinomy," he dealt with F. H. Bradley's brainteaser that "my body is only for nature" though nature is also for my body. The problem, as Sellars posed it, was that of the "relationship of the microcosm of the individual's experience with the macrocosm of reality," and his conclusion on the basis of all evidences was that "reality is stereometrical process with grades of organization and kinds of differentiation and, hence, degrees in selective reaction and influence. This in no wise [excludes the role of consciousness nor yet] conflicts with conservation."[4]

His essay on "A Fourth Progression in the Relation of Body and Mind" (1907)[5] confronted the problem head on. This was a widely informed essay in criticism of James Mark Baldwin's limitation of the alternative positions to three. Here indeed was Sellars' first quest of a "neglected alternative," a quest which was to continue to motivate him throughout his professional life. Sellars' work in this essay was preliminary, however, in spite of its fund of knowledge, and it would take us afield to analyze it here. He wrote a dozen substantial essays on this problem, one of them of fifty pages and two of them quite epochal.

The importance of this problem for Sellars' thought is further indicated by some of his statements about it. "The adequate handling of the mind-body problem," he wrote in 1938, "represents the synthetic stage of any philosophy, and it is at one and the same time a supreme test and indication of its power. Epistemology, ontology, and science must be marshalled together and all the essential terms of the problem must be defined and reintegrated."[6] "No problem is more crucial" to a philosophy "than the mind-body problem."[7] In this problem "nearly all critical questions can be seen to focus."[8] "I flatter myself," Sellars stated in his last major essay on the problem, "that some of my best work has been in connection with this question, the existential relation of consciousness to the mind-brain."[9]

Sellars' most interesting and epochal treatments of this problem center in three essays: "Is Consciousness Alien to the Physical?" (1916); "Evolutionary Naturalism and the Mind-Body Problem" (1920); and "The Double Knowledge Approach to the Mind-Body Problem" (1922). We shall focus on the essential ideas of these three essays, and conclude with some supplementation from "An Analytic Approach to the Mind-Body Problem," (1938), and "The Brain-Mind Situation. . . ." (1970). We start with "Is Consciousness Alien to the Physical?" because it assumes less than his earlier writings and is more rudimentary in its explanation. At the same time it is more definitive in its direction. It is actually his first systematic exposition of this problem.

The idea that consciousness is alien to the physical is quite specifically a modern intellectual stance. Consciousness has by no means always been thought of in opposition to the physical. It took the Greeks some time to recognize the difference between causal activity and sense perception. Sense perception had been for them immersed in the general activities of nature. Empedocles, with his doctrine that like perceived like, made perception a property of the elements though dependent on a relation between them. A similar hylozoism characterized the outlook of Heraclitus. Soul, he said, was the first principle, because it is a fiery vapor from which everything else is derived. Even in Plato and Plotinus, there was not a "hard and fast line between the intelligible world and matter. Matter [for Plotinus] does not exist independently of the one; it is the lower limit of emanation, the field of exhaustion, where being passes into non-being. We may [therefore] conclude that the mind-body dualism did not present itself in the same terms to the ancients as it does to the moderns."[10]

The influence of Christian theology on this problem is not dealt with here specifically by Sellars, i.e., the impact of such men as Origen, Augustine, Anselm, and Thomas. Later in his "Double Knowledge Approach to the Mind-Body Problem," he does distinguish the theological motive of a mind-body problem, stating that it was "influential from the beginning of *modern* philosophy,"[11] but that it is "not self-supporting and is logically secondary."[12]

The effect of religious thought on Descartes may be too easily overestimated but that it is increasingly there is evident in the difference between his *Discourse on Method* and his *Meditations*. That this difference is not merely one of "lip service" for the princes of the church is attested by two considerations: (1) the assumptions of the *Discourse;* (2) the fact that no case had yet been adequately made for the derivation of the mental (or spiritual) from the physical. Descartes, whatever the influences on him, defines the essences of body and mind in such a fashion that they have no actual community or basis for exchanges with each other. They were in principle strangers to each other. Hence the historically philosophical basis for the tradition that mind is alien to the body.

Sellars deals in three of his essays with the motives for the exclusion of the mind from the body. He is most succinct about these motives in "The Double Knowledge Approach to the Mind-Body Problem." We shall therefore sum up two of the motives on the basis of his treatment in that essay.

The first of these motives is epistemological. This motive for dualism "expresses itself in the assumption that the physical world is *exhaustively* revealed in the knowledge gained by the physical sciences," whereas the categories of science bespeak only "an approximation of its form or order" — not its essence.[13]

The second motive is categorial. This motive derives from "the disparity between the categories which characterize the content of knowledge gained by the physical sciences and the categories of introspective psychology. . . . The dominant effort in the past was to draw the whole of nature into the categories of mechanics. To do this for mind seemed impossible."[14] Descartes' drawing of the lines between mind and matter is the paradigm of this circumstance.

The third motive is methodological. In his *Evolutionary Naturalism*, Sellars distinguishes two phases of this motive. (1) The working dualism grew out of the data of sciences and consequent "ignoring of the nature of consciousness as relevant to the *content of knowledge*. The scientist's cognitive interest was in the physical world and not in consciousness."[15] A modification of this motive grew out of the actual state of the sciences up into the nineteenth century. As Sellars states:

> Science was for many years an investigation of inorganic masses. Only lately have the natural sciences gained a measure of autonomy and self-confidence enough to suggest new categories. And if the dominant sciences were physical and chemical and dealt below the level of the organism, it is not strange that the category of mind did not appear as involved in the data and their necessary interpretation. The absence of mind as a category is just what we should expect. . . . A sort of pragmatic dualism [consequently] grew . . . out of the state in which science was. Scientists did not feel that mind and consciousness were relevant to the physical world as they knew it.[16]

But this development belongs specifically to modern mechanistic thought. Even later science, Sellars urged, does not support the view that we have "intuitions" or immediate awarenesses of the substance or stuff of nature. It claims "a knowledge of the relative proportions, structure, relations, and functions of things. Space, either perceived or conceived, is not the substance of the physical."[17] Space is a relational category not an inherent quality or intrinsic possession.

The *behavior* of things, it was assumed, does not demand for its explanation the existence of the consciousness in them as an effective agent. We had long since passed from animism as a theory of nature to a more discriminating view. But we excluded the behavior of men and other animals from this view. Meanwhile biological and psychological sciences were developing naturally — as natural sciences. Does not their data seem to require the efficacy of conciousness as a natural, operative agency in certain types of things in certain circumstances? That Descartes did not recognize intelligence in animals is understandable from the paucity of animal studies in his time; but it also shows the relatively unempirical and doctrinaire nature of his stance. Recent studies indeed disclose that the "human organism is controlled by plans and memories" and that "there is no good reason to deny that something similar may hold of organisms less highly developed . . . a clear-sighted consideration of the argument from behavior is advantageous [in fact] because it forces us to remark the various grades of organization and of conduct in things."[18] This fact is preeminently important in the light of evolution.

This is not to deny distinctions between the mental and the

physical. We need indeed to obtain clear ideas of the usual contrasts between them to avoid being carried astray. Physical objects are not difficult to delimit. Those objects whose existence, structure, and relations we learn through the sense organs we take to be physical; while psychical entities are more difficult to demark. According to Sellars, "They do not possess that fundamental continuity which science has shown to be such a marked characteristic of the physical world."[19]

We may, however, distinguish two main classes of psychical objects: (1) those which have been thought to be physical but whose physical status has been denied (illusory or hallucinatory objects belong here, but so do such historically scientific entities as phlogiston); (2) those which are not physical and have made no claim to be physical—for instance, "A mathematical object . . . can be clearly conceived and analyzed, but we do not assign it a place among the things to which we may react bodily."[20] Sellars then asks:

> "What . . . is the nature of this systematic exclusion of psychical objects from the sphere of physical existence? Since it occurs in the mind, it is evidently not a dynamic expulsion from the space which physical things occupy [mathematical relations may indeed help us to understand the space of physical things]; rather is it the logical separation of classes of objects with different attributes and relations, and assigned to different spheres of existence. In other words, psychical objects are not excluded from the world as one physical thing excludes another. . . . The laws of behavior of the two realms are different . . . Who can think of a perfect triangle jostling an electron?"[21]

The logic of the first class of psychical objects — those that have for a time been accorded physical status — is accordingly different. But even they have not been mechanically expelled. They were not in fact excluded because they were psychical. They are considered psychical because they were found not to be actual, effective factors in the physical world, but ideas that people entertained for a time.

How does this distinction of psychical versus physical objects affect the question of the presence of consciousness in physical things? It does so negatively, at least. It eliminates the confusion of consciousness with its objects, says Sellars: "Consciousness is not an object in the usual sense of that term and, therefore, is not psychical when the psychical is defined as a class of objects distinguished from the class of physical objects."[22] There is thus no logical exclusion of consciousness from nature. It "does not claim a position in space as a *thing* in causal relation with other things. Nor is it an object with characteristics and relations which make its presence in nature meaningless."[23]

There are, however, two other usages of the term "psychical" which should be considered. One is its meaning as subjective, consisting of those feelings, ideas, and attitudes which are distinguishable from the object in the act of cognition. Its correlative *is* the objective. The contrast is thus between the psychical as subjective and whatever is objective, be it physical, mathematical, or otherwise public. The psychical as subjective is not excluded from the physical as physical but from the physical as objective. The physical, or at least some physical systems, may indeed include the subjective as part of their content of being. Finally, there is the meaning of the psychical as the personal, declares Sellars:

The individual has plans and purposes and values which are distinctly his own. He knows the common objective world, but uses it as a means for the furtherance of his own desires and ideas. The psychical is now the personal reference and control; it is the self as opposed to, yet in a working harmony with, the not-self. The not-self is not necessarily the physical; indeed, it is even more frequently, under the conditions of modern civilization, the social, another person or group of persons, a law, an obnoxious convention. . . . For our present problem the essential to realize is the coequal reality of these objects, be they physical things, wishes, the moral tone of the community, or my own plans. It is [thus] apparent that it is meaningless to speak of the exclusion of the personal by the physical. Here our practical knowledge is a challenge to theory. Feelings pulsate, and the face of the world is changed; ideas have hands and feet and force nature to do their will. The self and the not-self, the personal and the not-mine appear no more separated than one physical thing is separated from another. But how can this be? 'In the widest possible sense,' writes James, 'a man's Self is the sum total of all that he can call his; not only his body and his psychic powers, but his clothes and his house, his wife and children, his ancestors and friends, his reputation and works, his lands and horses, his yacht and bank-account.' To be sure, some selves are more modest, but the essential point is brought out by this question. It is this: The self is omnivorous and devours the physical equally with the undeniably psychical. The thinker who is seeking an existential line of demarkation between the self and the not-self is baffled by the seemingly capricious allotment of things to the two sides and by the shifting character of the boundary between them. A little reflection will, however, assure us that we have here a distinction which exists only within the field of the individual's experience. There is no reason why the self should not identify itself with various objects which have their representatives in the field. . . . [and] take possessive attitudes toward things which we experience. Such an attitude does not change the nature of things, but does alter our relations to them and may thus lead to the occurrence of overt actions. What I mean to assert is that the contrast between the self and the non-self is primarily within the individual's experience and has existential import only so far as it is the basis for conduct, personal or social. We may conclude, then, that the distinction does not coincide with that between the physical and consciousness and throws only a negative light upon it.[24]

"If [then] consciousness does not consist of psychical objects, nor of the subjective in contrast to the objective, nor of the prejudgmental flux of experiencing, nor of the personal, what is it?" asks Sellars. Is there a contrast, "still more primary, which has sometimes been confused with these and therefore misunderstood?" He continues:

In a preceding chapter we worked out a fairly definite conception of consciousness as identifiable with the whole field of the individual's experience. We saw that the realization of the unity and personal character of the total field is an achievement made by reflection in the face of the protests of meanings such as "common," "independent," and "permanent." Mental in this inclusive sense is a new meaning which has to gain clearness and mastery through a reflective struggle. As soon as this more critical standpoint is taken, the meanings and relations in which the different classes of objects are set are, like the objects which they qualify, seen to be mental. When this is done, another group of reflective meanings qualify the whole field of experience as such. It is judged to be a process whose parts are considered private and transient. It is this mental process which contains knowledge of existence independent of it. This way of approach to the total field of experiencing guards against the presuppositions of the sciences with which psychology is connected; and when philosophy uses the term 'consciousness' in relation to the mind-body problem, it should mean the mental in this inclusive sense in which it is identifiable with experiencing as a process.[25]

It is an interesting development, Sellars pointed out in 1916, that psychologists have enlarged their conception of man's mental life to connect consciousness with conduct. If, however, "consciousness is alien to the physical it is hard to comprehend why consciousness and conduct materially imply each other," Sellars observes.[26] The philosopher must take up this problem as it is found in science and "seek to understand [both] the reality studied by the physical sciences and of that studied by psychology" to discover "whether they are existentially separate,"[27] and, to the extent that this is so, how they can be or are related. We shall approach this question from the side of psychology.

"What are the characteristics of consciousness as brought out by psychology?" Sellars next asks. "There are at least four which are important for our problem. Consciousness is *personally toned;* it is synthetic; it is not directly observed; it is not a substance."[28]

Taking these characteristics in order, consciousness first of all has a "personal mooring. Any concept, however impersonal, is the thought of an individual and is bathed in a tide of feelings, purposes and desires . . ."[29] Mental pluralism is the law in this domain, and each stream of consciousness has an inner continuity or unity.

Secondly, consciousness is essentially synthetic. Any experience links itself, or tends to link itself, with all that is kindred to it. "Consciousness is alive with convection currents which bring every part to bear upon every other part."[30] At the same time consciousness is a stream which is continually changing. Hence consciousness is not directly conserved in the sense that the same experience presents itself repeatedly. We do not always realize, of course, that what we assign to the past is a creature of the present. The past is not literally revived. Consciousness thus is only indirectly conserved. When we say, however, that consciousness is indirectly conserved, Sellars claims, we mean that "our present experience would be different were it not for what we experienced in the past."[31] There is, in other words, a certain immanence of the past in the present.

We must, nonetheless, distinguish consciousness from mind. Continuity and growth are distinctive characteristics of mind: "The mind is like the score of some piece of music which the artist is seeking to perfect; consciousness, like the instrumentation of parts of it from time to time."[32]

Consciousness, thirdly, is not directly observable. We observe its objects, the foci of its attention and the backgrounds of these. But consciousness itself is never a direct object. It may be studied indirectly in terms of what it does and the sorts of "content" it entertains.

The last general characteristic of consciousness appears still more negative: consciousness is not a substance. It is not a thing to which the organism reacts, nor yet a thing which confronts the subject-self. It is a process of the self, hence a variant. As such it cannot be a substance; it is a function of a substance. As a function, it may act *in* things but not on things. Its action cannot be mechanical. Yet it may be efficacious as a process of something. It would be most significantly efficacious as a function of the brain.

This is not, in any way, to derogate from consciousness, which is extremely important to intelligent behavior and meaningful values. It is, however, to upgrade the brain as the organ of consciousness, that without which there would be no consciousness. It is to assert a two-phased relationship of substance and function. Since it is the very nature of substance, as we must now conceive it, to function, consciousness can be thought of, therefore, as integral to the "brain-mind."

When now, therefore, says Sellars, "we assert that consciousness is not alien to the physical world, we do not mean that feeling can be deduced by thought from motion or that a motion can become a feeling,"[33] but simply that these terms can be so conceived that they do not exclude each other. "The physical world may be extended and its parts have weight and yet be conscious, that is, have consciousness within it as part of its nature. The judgment of incongruity [between mind and physical substance] rests on a misunderstanding."[34] Yet not only are they not logically exclusive, they are evolutionarily intelligible as inclusive of each other. The physical world may rise to purposive activity and consciousness in certain organisms. Consciousness would thus be an immanently produced variant in a physical world.[35]

We are brought thus to what evolutionary naturalism has to offer toward resolution of the mind-body problem. Before elaborating this, however, we need to consider the types of relevant knowledge we have at our disposal and the consequent phenomena to be integrated. Sellars dealt with this in his "Double Knowledge Approach to the Mind-Body Problem."[36] What he did in this paper was, first, to synthesize the findings of the behaviorists, who were gaining increased recognition, with those of introspective experience whether in the laboratory or in common awarenesses. The behaviorists were claiming too much. Because all hard data seemed to be behavioral, some behaviorists had gone so far as to deny consciousness completely. But to deny consciousness is to deny our most immediate experience on the one hand and, secondly, to render epistemologically meaningless all our claims to knowledge. The positive findings of the behaviorists cannot, however, be ignored. They must be integrated with the wide range of data of inner experience: its sensory components, images, memories, perceivings, feelings, wishes, strivings, choices, hates, loves, conceptions, discursive thoughts. These inner experiences comprise one source and kind of knowledge. External observation, whether of behavior or of simple physiognomy and geography, is another type. As Sellars explained: "Thus the knowledge gained by physical science is inevitably *external to its object* in this sense that it grasps only those characteristics which are reproducible in another medium . . . it cannot reach a literal intuition of, or participation in, the life or energies of the thing known. But . . . within this subjective medium, knowledge of its own content can arise [its sense data, feeling tones, memories, ideas, desires, etc.] Here we have the two kinds and directions of knowledge,"[37] with seemingly different objects. And to understand the human organism, *both are necessary.*

The lack of simple equivalence in objects is "explicable by the nature and reach of the two kinds of knowledge." One arises in the "filling" or content of the active brain, claims Sellars, and "inspects *quales* there present; the other deciphers the characteristics of the brain as a body by means of the cognitive value of certain sense-data. It is because consciousness is not a 'thing,' or 'stuff,' but a structured complex of *quales* that a relation of partial identity, or inclusion, can be conceived . . . Thus it is only by doing justice to both sets of categories and to the two kinds of data of the two kinds of knowledge that a solution of the mind-body problem is made possible."[38]

It is this relationship of subjective content to a special physical organ, or system of organs, that is meant by the term "minded brain." The naturalistic support for such an agency is evolutionary and emergent. In the preceding chapter we have already dealt with the cosmological drama of emergent substances. To this process of emergence we now return.

For our purposes in this chapter, the thesis of evolutionary naturalism is this: "The living organism, when properly and adequately conceived, includes consciousness and is the sole source of that differential behavior which distinguishes it from less integrated bodies";[39] and it is a very special emergent, over a vast history, among bodies or substances. The essential feature of Sellars' conception of emergent evolution is the intrinsic relation between novel organization and novel existence with novel properties or qualitative content. All evolutionists believe that conscious organisms were at one time a very novel existence.

What import now has the disclosure concerning emergent evolution for the mind-body problem? It has a preeminent import since it shows that we are not dealing with two things, but with one entity and its functions. Consciousness, as William James said, is a function, but he was equivocal about what consciousness was a function of. In one strand of his psychology he treated it in essentially its own terms. In another strand he treated it as a function of the organism. But in his essay, "Does Consciousness Exist?" he presents consciousness as a function of a neutral something which he calls "pure experience." Yet he concludes the essay by characterizing thinking in the physiological terms of breathing.

What then is consciousness a function of? We have, in fact, three sets of data; two of them are data of objective observation and the third is introspective. In his "Double Knowledge Approach to the Mind-Body Problem," Sellars proceeds to demonstrate the correlation between external and introspective data, and to argue cogently that they are two sides of the same coin: the coin in this instance being that terrifically complex evolutionary product, the "minded brain." To treat consciousness as other than the functioning of the brain in certain notable operations is to multiply entities and to have the historically impossible problem of envisioning their relationship. Man may have his 950 or so vestigial organs, but he was not thrown together in the fashion that Descartes has been found to imply.

I mentioned that there are two kinds of external data to be taken into account with respect to the brain-mind unity. There are the data of behavioral observation and that of neurophysiological observation (and the neural and otherwise physiological may again be separated). Suffice it to indicate that Sellars' conception of the mind was enlarged by the behaviorists with whom he virtually grew up philosophically at the University of Michigan. The mind became a term of wider import than "consciousness" which is a term to which behaviorists have difficulty in giving meaning. Mind, however, has behavioral meaning. It is a term for certain occurrent dispositions and/or tendencies and for actions expressive of the unity of an organism. To Sellars mind came to include integrative, interpretative, and directive capacities of the brain.

But he also had discourse with physiologists, neurologists, and social psychologists. The story of his interchanges with scientists is still to be compiled. Most important, I believe, for the mind-body issue are his consultations with the neurologists, such as Sherrington, Lord Brain, and C. Judson Herrick. Regarding Herrick's 1956 publication, *The Evolution of Human Nature*, Sellars wrote:

> I had the opportunity of talking it over with him in its first, manuscript form. He has always been . . . an advocate of the unified action of the organism as

a whole as against fixed reflexes. Herrick has always been interested in philosophy. I think this helped him to avoid the retention of dualism, something Sherrington retained. The brain was the organ of behavior but of a guided behavior on which intelligence had leverage. He and I agreed on the role of learning as enlarging the stimulus-response circuit. The shift to this as the 'open' unit which gave a setting to both stimulus and response represented the basic reorientation in the causal theory of perception.[40]

Perception thus becomes one of the significant functions of the brain-mind; yet, as we have seen, it is built around relevant behavior.

The brain likewise functions in explicitly conscious activities. The behaviorists from Watson to Skinner are wrong in their rejection of consciousness. Skinner, for instance, holds that the neurologist will never find mental objects in the nervous system. As Norman Melchert notes, a neurosurgeon cannot by cutting human tissues discover a pain. But he may find an abrupt response by the patient which the patient describes as a pain, and the surgical operator may, when he himself is a patient, come to know what sort of thing a pain is, introspectively as well as neurologically. The surgeon has his own internal indices. The behaviorist, too, if he had but taken more pains with the accomplishments of his behavior, would have had his own pains as unpleasant and sometimes excruciating evidences.

The whole business of correlating factors and interpreting the correlated data makes sense in terms of evolved entities with highly specialized capacities: to sense, to feel, to be aware of things and states, to desire, to recall, to have images, to use symbols, to conceive, to think reflectively, and to reach conclusions. All of these capacities develop in biological contexts, even though it is more than possible that some of them jump ahead of biological needs and, not at all infrequently, interfere with the satisfaction of biological demands. (Our capacities to use drugs that sooner or later destroy our bodies is a particularly relevant type of instance.) But the whole range of possibilities for the elaboration of mathematical, philosophical, and imaginative systems also lies open to the human organism. Sellars is in no sense a reductionist. All the possibilities of experience and thought that people claim — and sometimes, at least, misinterpret — are available to humans, but as organic functions. The foundations of philosophy, for example, reside, in the first instance, in the human organism. And a philosophy is not only incomplete but significantly irrelevant which does not allow for this basis.

Sellars has thus clearly passed from body to mind and back again in his solution of the mind-body problem. His solution accords with the latest achievements in science, including cybernetics. And it is noteworthy that he is the forerunner of what Norman Melchert calls "a whole rash of identity theories" of mind-body relationship.[41] That others of note are still clinging to the cliffs overhanging this historical chasm is no evidence against the adequacy of Sellars' theory. The causeway is there for all to use who are not impeded by preconceptions that obscure their intellectual vision.

We are now ready to undertake our rounding out of Sellars' work on this problem. Philosophically it was a preeminently focal problem, involving, as he held it does, epistemology, ontology, and science — and even lyric experience. It is an especially good instance indeed of the importance of science for philosophy. We have noted in Chapters 2 and 3 that scientific method and scientific findings are not enough. Philosophy must complete science, by giving its categories a setting and an ontology. There is, however, a filling-out function which science can perform for philosophy, a giving of detail to the conceptual picture. This is illustrated by the dramatic story of the emergence of the conditions of life on the earth and the actual production of life by Miller and Fox. It is less dramatically supported by the new developments in science which accrued during Sellars' early professional years: (1) the questioning of the adequacy of the laws of mechanics for any but molar masses; (2) the increased recognition of the empirical autonomy of the diverse sciences; (3) the admission of creative synthesis in nature with accompanying critical points and new properties; (4) the rise of behaviorism as a physical science bringing human conduct into the physical world.[42] Later, Sellars called attention to the role of Gestalt psychology in showing both the physiological and psychological importance of structure or pattern for the qualitative developments we find in the world. We have also, earlier in this chapter, paid our respects to the neurologists. The story of Sellars' debt to scientists, I repeat, has only been suggested. Yet science itself, however meaty, rigorous, and precise, is not enough. Epistemology enters to show the piecemeal and contingent nature of science, the types of knowledge humans have, the respective roles of these modes of knowledge, their limits and their plausibilities, yet their complementary functions. Epistemology attempts indeed to show in what ways we can claim to have knowledge at all and to what extent. An adequate theory of the minded-brain must account for knowledge, not only of its types and objects but also of itself, i.e., of knowledge of knowledge.

Ontology likewise enters to treat such questions as the existential status of consciousness. What sorts of things are functions and what are they functions of? May there not be special kinds of substances of which consciousness is a function? And may not some living organisms be that kind of substance? The question of the efficacy of consciousness in such a circumstance enters here, and we must discuss that question. But first there enters another quite interesting question as to the where of consciousness, if consciousness is a function of the organism, or more specifically of its brain.

Sellars claims that consciousness is *in the brain*. Others have criticized this claim. Some have even gone so far as to assert that consciousness is so free an agent that it can reach out and traverse the stars. They cannot, of course, mean this literally unless they are such pure idealists that they regard the stars as a special set of mental entities—and such extravagances must surely be discounted.

But what does Sellars mean by saying that consciousness is in the brain? He does not mean that it is physically contained within the brain as a pea is in its pod, or even as a mouse is in a trap. Consciousness is not trapped. It is an expression of the special dynamics of the brain, and it is in the brain more in the sense that the sharpening of a knife is in the whetstone or the light is in the candle. Consciousness is a natural function of a special organization of nerve tissues. It is adjectival or adverbial. It is a quite special property of the brain when it is intelligently or discriminatingly at work. It is the brain's awareness notably in non-routine situations and in calculating relevant or adequate courses of action. Consciousness is in the brain as its unique functions are in nerve tissue and organic substance. It enables the organism to reach out intelligently to things though it does not by itself reach out to anything.

How, then, can consciousness have effects or be efficacious? Sellars made an interesting reply to James B. Pratt on this question.[43] Pratt, evidently, could not envisage consciousness as having effects without operating on the brain as an agency on the outside. But Sellars was not talking about efficacy in the sense of the effects of one thing *upon* another. He was talking in terms of immanent causality, which we illustrated in the last chapter by the effects of a hormone within an organism. The stimulus for the glandular activity may be within the organism itself: a thought, a cumulative ingredient in the blood, organic growth or deterioration, etc. Consciousness operates in similar fashion. The causal reality is not consciousness by itself but "conscious physiological process." Consciousness is not required to insert itself into the brain.

Consciousness is a special level of functioning by or of the brain, declares Sellars: "No; we have here to do with immanent causality."[44]

"I believe," writes Sellars, "that consciousness emerges *with* nervous organization for the reason that I hold it to be intrinsic to it, that is, internally related in the manner I have indicated." It yields or gives that special content of being in which humans participate firsthand. "As to what *content of being* physiological events have below this [human] level, we can have no intuitive knowledge because we cannot participate in them. But I see no reason to hold that such events do not contain an internal content of a qualified sort, perhaps some dimly felt urgency. But our situation is such that we cannot share in it. . . ."[45]

When we come to man "the knower, self-conscious artist, and scientist," we know that we have two views of being: from the inside as well as from the outside. We know that we have here indeed a being who, in Heideggerian terms, has his own being as a problem. Humans constitute indeed "a critical point in nature and the thought of nature. . . . [Man] has a kind of self-knowledge which is not reducible to external observation. . . . Can it be denied [indeed] that all an individual's *experiencings* have a disclosure-capacity for himself as a continuing creature?"[46]

Consciousness, however, is not identical with being minded, and we have compared mind to a musical composition. Consciousness, we have said, is its occasional instrumentation. From the standpoint of "the double-knowledge and emergence solution of the mind-body problem,"[47] mind is a term for the integrative, interpretive, and directive capacities and functions of the human brain; hence for certain operational dispositions, capacities, and cumulative readinesses which may rise to consciousness in certain circumstances. Basically, mind is a physical category. The mental level of life is that of intelligent behavior, but intelligent behavior can frequently be instinctive and habitual. It need not be conscious. But when the organism is confronted by new types of circumstances with significant variations in its situation, instinctive and habitual behavior is not enough. In man and certain other organisms mind arises to discriminating and problem-solving consciousness in instances that are not routine. And consciousness can enlarge and deepen to encompass all possible experiencings. Consciousness is not, like mind, a physical category or system but a "*qualitive Dimension of the existential content of a highly involved physical system.*"[48] Consciousness encompasses the content and processes of experience.

Consciousness is private. We cannot experience each other's feelings or thoughts. Yet there are persons who are not adept at concealing their mental states. And this failure itself is revealing, showing the naturally close relation between consciousness and expressive behavior. Though we cannot directly intuit another's thought or feeling, we can read experience via behavior and respond more or less relevantly. People can communicate expressively. This, however, is knowledge by indirection, and not always the knowledge we may take it to be.

The term "unconscious mind" has clear meaning from Sellars' standpoint. Sellars' findings therefore fit in with depth psychology as well as with behaviorism and Gestalt structuralism. Organization is a rar-reaching factor in this system, but it is always the organization of something. Basically it is the organization of somethng substantial, i.e., some form of substance.

Sellars is thus the formulator of an identity theory of the brain-mind relation, and forerunner of a sizable number of such theories. But to call it an identity theory may seem too delimiting. Sellars has more accurately said: "The perspective which was opening up for me was, I thought, best indicated by the rather cumbersome description: *the double-knowledge and emergence solution of the mind-body problem.*"[49] This places no limit on the possibilities in the life of either the mind or the body. The life of the mind in fact expresses the possibilities in the life of the body. It would be simpler, however, to call it the theory of the minded-brain.

CHAPTER 5

Critical Naturalism in Values

MAN is not merely a perceiver and knower, even with a great deal of action thrown in. He is a valuing being: liking, desiring, cherishing, aspiring, appraising, ascribing, choosing, achieving, perfecting, disposing. In Sellars' words, the "terrific sweep and range of the self as a living, effective and conative thing . . . makes it an ongoing microcosm immerged in the tides of being and aware of their situational impact"[1] — hence, all sorts of value responses to all kinds of things: entities, persons, groups, ideas, projects, objectives. "Anything which we desire, need, want, or enjoy either for its own sake or as a means" may be a value, Sellars says.[2] But things that we think we ought to want are values, and they are often considered of basic importance. Valuation is more, in fact, than desiring or enjoying, according to Sellars: "What we may call attitude, decision . . . or evaluative judgment stands out."[3]

Valuation is an integral part of the process of living. It enters into our rudimentary perceptions, since these arise to serve the survival and development of the organism and only become disinterestedly specialized when the pressures of growth and survival are no longer primary. Meanwhile values become demarked in terms of the kinds of satisfactions or other increments which they yield: organic, intellectual, aesthetic, moral, societal, religious, etc. The wealth and the shadings of values are vast. Human living is a great value enterprise.

I

In view of these considerations it is indeed surprising that the question of a general theory or philosophy of value had to wait until the nineteenth century to gain recognition as a primary quest. Plato, in his *Philebus*, indeed attempted a general inquiry into the good simply as good, raising the question whether the good was thought or pleasure and concluding that there was something higher than both, e.g., the measure or standard. And religious philosophers, on an essentially Platonic base, proceeded to account for good as an infusion of being from a supernal source. But the attempt to work out such a philosophy on empirical grounds is largely a twentieth-century development.

There are indeed two strands in the development of value theory: an Hegelian strand issuing in such work as Bernard Bosanquet's *Individuality and Value* and an empirical strand stemming from the nineteenth-century Austrian philosopher Franz Brentano. The latter's theme in ethics was that right and wrong are the expressions of right loves and right hates. These emotions, for him, had a noetic character. They were or could be insighted types of experience, comparable to what he took to be the self-evidence of certain propositions in mathematics and logic. The point of importance for our purposes, however, is that right and wrong are empirical qualities, and that such value experiences derive from the relevance of the objective references of feelings.

Two of Brentano's students, Alexius von Meinong and Christian von Ehrenfels, divided on whether values were objects of feeling or of desire, Meinong insisting on feeling, Ehrenfels on desire. But for both values were to be found in experience.

The American philosopher Ralph Barton Perry showed that both of these positions could be combined in the conception of value as "any object of any interest." Interest may be primarily a matter of likes and dislikes as feelings, or it may be first and foremost a matter of desire. There is an instinctive, organic basis for interest, however, and one can therefore find a connection between feeling and desire. Yet it is Stephen Pepper, rather than Perry, who has best shown that feeling and desire are features of a single process and the presumed issue between them is a false one.

We must add one more name to the immediate background of Sellars' theory — John Dewey. It would involve us in too much duplication of discussion to bring in G. E. Moore here, though Moore's ethical position was one to which Sellars responded most critically. Dewey's is closer to Sellars. Dewey added an experimentalist, problem-solving, and dominantly social base to the theory of value. He distinguished actual functional ends from end-in-view and found reliable values to be functions of judgments rather than of bare interests *per se*.

Where now against this background does Sellars' value-theory fit?

First of all, his earliest writings specifically on values appeared the same year as Perry's *General Theory of Value*, 1926, when Sellars published an article in *Philosophical Review* on "Cognition and Valuation" and a series of chapters on "Human Life and Values" in his *Principles and Problems of Philosophy*. By 1920, moreover, he had already written a preface to his wife's translation of Bouglé's *Evolution of Values*. Other writings date from 1932 ("The Nature and Status of Values")[4] to 1967 ("In What Sense Do Value Judgments Have Objective Import?").[5] In between are two essays "Can A Reformed Materialism Do Justice to Values?"[6] and "Valuational Naturalism and Moral Discourse,"[7] with other papers still to be published.

As in epistemology and ontology, Sellars' work on value theory has the stamp of his quite independent thought and inquiry. His view is sharply distinguished from some of his predecessors and contemporaries while having various affinities with others. He is, for example, directly opposed to the value theories of transcendental idealists. Values are the objects of human (or animal) valuations and do not obtain apart from these valuings. There is no Platonic realm of ideal values, according to Sellars. Value theory, therefore, from Hegel to Bosanquet and Urban, and their successors, is on the wrong course. True, Sellars did find merit in DeWitt Parker's position, and we shall note this at the appropriate point. But the merit was not in Parker's transcendentalism; it was, rather, in the process of personal valuing.

Sellars likewise was quite sweepingly opposed to G. E. Moore's non-naturalism and intuitionism. Moore's claim that good is an indefinable and irreducible quality, like yellow, is so familiar that explanations would be tedious. Assertions that good is happiness or pleasure or well-being are instances of the naturalistic fallacy. One can always ask of each of these: "But is it really good?" Good is known intuitively for what it is. No further analysis is possible.

But, says Sellars, Moore has approached values as things to be known, rather than as functions of things to be appraised or evaluated. He had not the background to comprehend the roles of value objects in human economy. And his faith in intuition ignores the ways in which different people's intuitions are opposed to each other. "Intuition" may be a suggestive source of ideas, when it is adequately informed, but it is not the certification of anything.

Comparably, with the non-cognitivists and their view that values are in essence the envincings of feelings, the problem of value is one of definition in relationship to knowledge. With their pure cognitivism in logic and science — and cognition conceived in terms of verifiability — valuations have no cognitive base. Sheer feeling is their actual foundation. Assessments or appraisals of function cannot enter, though persuasion may affect our beliefs. That there may be realistic grounds for persuasion is a factor that carries us to another group of analysts, the "good reasons" group. Suffice it here to indicate that the failure to distinguish between the practical reason of justifiable appraisals and the reason of the logic of proof leaves the non-cognitivists in an artificial and frustrating limbo. To be unable to justify any appraisals is to be unable to act with informed conviction.

The problem of both Moore and the non-cognitivists stems from their failure to distinguish valuation, as appraisal of role or function of any sort of object in reference to human living, from cognition as disinterested knowing. Valuation is interested assignment or ascription of value, but it can be intelligently informed, declares Sellars:

> In cognition we hold ourselves aloof from objects and restrain those direct relations and interests which are characteristic of living. In short . . . we temporarily inhibit desires and activities which are directed toward objects in a concrete participative way and try to understand what they are, what their structure and properties should be conceived as. On the contrary, in the usual run of living we are agents adjusting ourselves to the things around us, using, avoiding, and enjoying them. . . . In living we have no sense of abrupt separation between ourselves and things. We cooperate with other persons, we handle objects, we move them, alter them, enjoy them. We are *with* things. Action emphasizes our relations with the world, while cognition emphasizes our distinctness so far as existence is concerned.[8]

Knowing, of course, is an important condition and ingredient in sound evaluations. But "we value objects that we know by means of additional data irrelevant to knowledge as such. . . . Our feelings, desires, and interests are conditions of the assignment of value to an object,"[9] and they are objectively referential rather than the objects of value themselves. The issue is the assignment of values that best bespeak the roles of objects in the human economy, broadly considered.

Perry, Parker, and Dewey are three value philosophers for whom Sellars had some affinity. With his conception of value as "any object of any interest," Perry recognized the double basis of values; but with his mechanistic conception of knowing he established no proper connection between the object and the interest of the subject — and indeed played down the object in the value equation.

Parker reversed Perry's equation. Instead of values as objects of interests, interests themselves were the values. Values were thus subjective phenomena.

Now why should Sellars be deferential to a spokesman for a subjectivistic theory of values? The answer is partly that Parker was Sellars' own eminent colleague at the University of Michigan. But it was also because there is a large half-truth in the subjectivist emphasis, which Sellars acknowledges:

> It calls attention to the basis [of valuation] in the self which, of course, must be recognized. The materialist does not dispute this fact, but has a different conception of the self than has the panpsychist. . . . It is clearly a defensible idea that the organized and operative organic self is conscious and that such consciousness is a 'natural isolate' from a context of functioning in which it participates. Here, and here alone, is the individual on the inside of nature. It would [thus] seem that the cortex is qualitied in this participative fashion, even though abstract descriptive knowledge using sensory evidence, as a point of departure, cannot attain it from the outside. . . . The self is a continuant which we reflexively denote and categorially know even while, in consciousness, participating in it. . . .
>
> The wide varieties of values reflect the bearing of the object upon the self. The aesthetic object connects up with different interests and attitudes than does the object used as a tool. The personal status called 'fame' evokes different tendencies than does health or wealth. . . . It is the self which is the center and which relates objects and objectives in manifold ways according to their known capacities and relevancies. . . .
>
> It may, to some, seem strange that a materialist should so emphasize the self and call attention to its configurated and balanced interplay of interests and admirations as the decisive source of appraisals. But the philosophical materialist is an empiricist, though a realistic one. He sees no reason not to acknowledge the fact that the human, organic, self is gifted with the capacity of cognitive reference and appraisal and that, in self-consciousness, interests and admirations induce value judgments upon all that can be thought of as having a bearing upon the economy and aspirations of the self. Expressions, frustrations, interdependence, relative autonomy — all affect the pattern of valuation. Here our categories must be those of life itself, but of a life evolved to the stage of judgment and self-consciousness.[10]

Parker's stress is, accordingly, an important one if unrealistically conceived. Sellars, however, has more in common with Dewey than with either Perry or Parker. Not only are they both naturalistic and antitranscendentalist in their conception of values, without being simply mechanistic in their respective naturalisms, but they both regard value judgments as the key to reliable values. Liking, desiring, or holding dear is not enough; there must be conscious appraisals in the light of relevant factors. "Dewey," said Sellars, "had a keen sense for critical and experimental valuations but assumes that values are features of that blanket experience within which his thinking operates."[11] His difficulty was his lack of an adequate realism. His actual realism, apart from his social interactionism, was a perspective realism according to which everything that happens answers to objective conditions of some variety. Yet all is within experience. His experimentalism is a process of problem-solving within a general matrix which he called "experience." Dewey had an unduly skimpy ontology with which to give substance or body to his value theory, but he also had need of the recognition of the subjective as such. Sellars explains, "Were Dewey to give greater recognition to the subjective and to admit the framework of physical realism, and were Parker to advance from his Berkeleian subjectivism, they would, I anticipate, meet at about the point to which the argument of this paper leads, namely, that value assignments are objective after their kind and express the significance of objects and events to the interests and admirations of the self."[12]

In valuation, "a peculiar reflexive story [is] added to the cognitional framework" and has its own "kind of objective significance."[13] "Good reasons" are adducible for certain value appraisals, and Sellars finds the "good reasons" analysts to be contributing importantly to the recognition of the objective conditions of value judgments. My own thought regarding these analysts is that they are still involved in a haze of usages, and a great deal of systematic realistic work remains to be done.

Meantime the work of a down-to-earth axiologist, Stephen C. Pepper, has gained too little attention; I refer to his *Sources of Value*. There, on the basis of psychological and other studies, he distinguishes a number of selective systems as frames of value reference. Single purposive structures, as in hunger or sex, may in certain circumstances constitute one type of selective value system. But fear or hate may repress either hunger or sex, or some combination of other drives may do the repressing. In actual "life-space," indeed, we have such conflicts of motives and groups of motives, and the "life-space" of the combinations and conflicts of motives is a second type of selective system taking precedence over single purposive drives. The individual's personal situation is just such an alignment of interests and motives in specific circumstances.

The personality structure is a third system with its organization of habits and dispositions. Pepper treats the personality structure as a defensive integration, protecting the individual from anything that might militate against its special pattern. Actually it has long been treated as a system striving for its own self-fulfillment. The "life-space" of drives under special circumstances is different from the pattern of sentiments and habits that constitutes the central thrust of personality. Hence personality structure is an important selective system or frame of value reference.

Fourthly, the social situation is frequently a selective system. It used to be that juvenile delinquency could be dealt with as a purely local affair. Now with our mass media, it is often impossible to do this. But there are domestic and other local problems which can be dealt with in terms of a quite limited set of social circumstances. A family or village may indeed handle some of its problems without reference beyond the immediate group.

Finally there is the cultural pattern, comprised of institutions, social habits, and values that constitute the way of life of a society or people. The cultural pattern functions to safeguard the group against anything from the outside or inside that threatens its modus vivendi. Positively, it is the way a society envisages the achievement of its espoused values.

Now, there are natural norms within each of these selective systems and principles of legislation between these systems. The quiescence of a purposive structure following the attainment of its appropriate object is such a natural norm, whereas under social pressure the cultural pattern tends strongly to legislate over purely individual preferences. The case between the selective systems is not always by any means this simple, but this naturalistic type of analysis gives a factual basis for a "good reasons" diagnosis. My contention is that the "good reasons" value theories need more of this natural analysis to give a realistic quality to their arguments and to show what values mean immanently in life.

Sellars, indeed, with his own social and institutional emphases, parallels Pepper or, conversely, Pepper extends Sellars' analyses. Sellars does not begin with single purposive structures, though he assumes them; comparably with Pepper, he does start — as one point of departure — with behavioral, experimental psychology. The personal introspective experience is another point of departure and here we find the issues of "life-space" and the personal situation.

The importance of the organic self gets quite different special stressing from Sellars, and there is no doubt that it is for him a primary frame of value reference. Few philosophers, moreover, have been more conscious than Sellars of the complications to individual lives due to social situations. But it is to institutional and cultural factors as well as to personality that Sellars was especially attentive. We shall defer treatment of those factors to our presentation of his social philosophy in Chapter 7.

Value judgments, in any case, for Sellars are "justifiable in terms of their relevant bases."[14] The self is affected by objects with respect to its vital tendencies and desires, and the social situation is a conditioner of these tendencies and desires. Values are created by the responsible relations of the life in which they are immersed. Cognition gives the framework within which the self embroiders its appraisals. The "self moves back and forth within the structure deciphered by cognitive activity, working out consequential, reflexive valuations," says Sellars.[15] Values are not pressed on man from the outside. They reflect and express relevances — the functional import of objects, proposals, persons, etc. for the personal and social economy or way of life. The well-being of the individual, and of all individuals in their socio-cultural worlds, is the ultimate justification of value appraisals.

Valuations can have meaning from one person to another because of the common denominators of human selves: the dislike of frustration, demand for happiness, the capacity for loyalty and admiration, to mention just some. The plasticity of human nature is limited; reliable appraisals of objects will accordingly be significantly similar. Values bespeak the responses of high-level organs to objective conditions.

To sum up regarding general value theory:

1) Axiology can, therefore, be clarified only after ontology and epistemology have given a firm structure to philosophic thought.

2) Values are objectively conditioned and pertain to objects — actual and possible — in the light of their bearing upon individuals and groups.

3) Value judgments are justifiable rather than true in a cognitional sense.

4) The expression "intrinsic values" is misleading — why not merely speak of "satisfactions?"

5) "Terminal values" can be contrasted with "instrumental values."[16] A terminal value is in the nature of a commitment.

6) Value judgments can be communicated but, because of their reflexive base, involve personal shadings.

7) There are levels of emergent teleology, only the highest of which involve ends-in-view.

8) Logical positivism rightly rejects value transcendentalism but does not do justice to cognitional reference or objective appraisal.

9) Though they have one base in moral sentiments, Sellars sees no reason to reduce ethical concepts to nonethical ones. Such factual subjectivism ignores objective appraisals. Moral emotions and attitudes are both referential and empirically conditioned.

10) Ontological materialism does not imply "ethical materialism." Reformed materialism, by its recognition of causal levels in nature and its forthright realistic empiricism, can do justice to what is unique in human personality and in the play of human values.

II

It is one merit of Sellars' position that it takes account of the total range of human values: purely personal values, values in ordinary practical experience, values of highly sensitive and creative experience, ideal as well as immediate values, and the more sophisticated values of the initiated and critical.

Morality and religion are areas in which Sellars dealt in special realms of value. Aesthetics was not his province; it was the specific field of his colleague DeWitt Parker. Yet Sellars has a section on "Value in Aesthetic Experience" in his *Principles, Perspectives, and Problems of Philosophy.*[17]

"Those who have devoted themselves to an analysis of the aesthetic experience," he writes, "emphasize its unhurried, contemplative character. He who enjoys a landscape, for instance . . . is not trying to do something practical, to estimate the quality of the soil, the geological character of the rocks, the distance from town. Rather is he aware of color harmonies, delightful blendings of perspectives that satisfy."[18]

He then proceeds to quote Bernard Bosanquet that "the simplest aesthetic experience is to begin with a pleasant feeling . . ."[19] And as the experience develops it has three characteristics: it is a stable feeling, a relevant feeling, and a common feeling. Bosanquet writes, in summary, "so far the aesthetic attitude seems to be something like this; preoccupation with a pleasant feeling, embodied in an object which can be contemplated, and so obedient to the laws of an object, and by an object is meant an appearance present to us through perception or imagination."[20]

Sellars amplifies, maintaining that "we are concerned with the object as it appears in our experience as a sensuous presentation capable of evoking and absorbing certain elements in our nature. Aesthetic contemplation is not passive but creative. And in art we mold objects until they express as perfectly as possible what we demand in the way of form, order, and harmony. . . . The aim of art is . . . to create something delightful and expressive."

Then Sellars quotes Buermeyer's statement that "the aesthetic object is such a reorganization of conventional impressions . . . as will reveal their distinctive significance for feeling or emotion."[21] And he also quotes from Parker: "Hence the artist infuses into the world which he creates a new and wholly subjective simplicity and unity *to which there is no parallel in nature.*[22]

"Art," states Sellars, "springs out of human living and deepens it. . . . Man is a child of nature to the full, while possessed of the capacity to create works of art which improve upon nature in their emotional appeal." In cognizing *per se,* we inhibit for the time our practical relations with things, and even in the aesthetic attitude there is something of this withdrawal. It has been called "psychical distance."[23] There is in the aesthetic moment, as Arnold states, much more than the immediate sensuous object; there are all the meanings and overtones with which the aesthetic subject may surround it, from the richness of his background.

Ethics

Sellars is again on his own in ethics. Because of his special social interest, ethics is a matter of basic concern. Moral issues and values arise in the process of human living together. As Harold A. Bosley points out regarding the emergence of the Ten Commandments, living at close quarters in the wilderness for many years presented acute problems to the Israelites.[24] The stern prescriptions of the Commandments were directed to those problems. The locus of ethics within socio-political philosophy has of course been shown by Aristotle, Hobbes, and others. Morality is, in the first place, social. It is a matter of the regulation and direction of conduct in a social setting.

Morality therefore, at least in its earliest stages, takes the form of rules for living. "People living in groups could not get along together without rules and standards," observes Sellars. Moral rules are indeed inevitable; the problem is to make them adequate.

Yet rules, it has been found, are not enough. "They must be backed by attitudes and concern," argues Sellars.[25] And they must find focus in principles. It is interesting, therefore, that in this age of presumed ethical sophistication, the concern about moral rules has returned. Is this a regression to a more primitive type of ethics? Or is it a recognition that while *ethics* rises to the standpoint of principles, the practice of morality revolves generally around rules? Socially our *prima facie* duties can be stated as rules.

Yet the moral point of view is not simply or primarily a matter of rules. Sellars agrees with Kurt Baier here that the moral point of view is one of action on principle when it is in the interests of everyone to act on principle rather than on personal self-interest. We must indeed distinguish between the socially prudential man (who may be a politician) and the man who has the moral standpoint. The moral point of view is "objective, transpersonal, and universal in intention," says Sellars.[26]

The context of morality is that of human agency, with its responsibilities as well as its prerogatives. Morality bespeaks a high level of efficient causality, that of agential causality. "Human beings are moral agents in a social setting. This setting has its requirements and its developments."

The moral point of view centers specifically in such conceptions as right and wrong, duty and obligation. These have elements of requiredness about them, in contrast to the concept of good which, as Dewey has pointed out, has more of the element of attraction than of demand. It is thus no accident that morality has been prescriptive, and often in the form of commands.

But the specifically moral categories function in the *overall* control of human values. Morality "works within human life as a whole and what are called its non-moral values." It thus involves or relates to the categories of good and goods, and it does so in a number of ways. There are indeed specifically moral goods, such as virtues, good motives and good character. But these are moral goods in the light of their roles in making life an approvable kind of thing in its various contexts. In one sense, therefore, morality may be said to be concerned with adequate achievement in men's patterns of values, hence with the organization of all types of value. In its stricter realistic sense it involves choices between grouped combinations of both goods and bads. The phrase "axiological ethics" is therefore appropriate.

The specifically moral point of view expresses a society's sense of what is required to achieve and maintain in a satisfactory way its pattern of life. There is, in consequence, a stress on moral rules as modes of right conduct and on obligation as that which is mandatory for the realizing in this society of an adequate kind of life.

There is, accordingly, a truth in both the utilitarian and the deontologist's ethical positions. "Right" and "duty" express the consciousness of the requirednesses for a way of life in a society or culture. Institutions, including morality itself, arise to articulate and effect these necessities. The sense of obligation is "prepared for in morality as a social institution." This is the kernel of truth in the deontologist's ethics, but the deontologists "seem to assume that moral intuition" is not only adequately self-justifying but that it also "carries with it its own source of moral motivation," says Sellars. "Deontological theories have a strong sense of moral laws and the primacy of duty" but they "seem to lack any well-worked-out idea of the nature of moral thinking."[27]

Right and duty, genetically and in actual function, are directed toward the well-being of people in a society and to the welfare of the society itself. Morality is justified teleologically by the way of life it furthers. A whole pattern of life is involved. "Moral rules arise and are validated in the business of life," and the business of life is carried on in a cultural context. The welfare of the persons in this pattern of living is the validating factor. Utilitarianism represents this emphasis on consequential welfare. It did not do justice to the requirements inherent in a society's pattern of life or the imperative components of moral agency, but its teleological consciousness is a basic credit. Morality is for man, and only in that sense is man also for morality.

Sellars disposes of the other variously one-sided "ethical" isms. Ethical subjectivism is socially irresponsible. Ethical intuitionism does not stand up; it is anarchic. Psychological hedonism takes satisfactions or pleasures to be ends in themselves rather than indications of what is generally good for the organic self. It thus loses "sight of primary interests of a sustaining kind," and of the "indicational" function of pleasure. Ethical relativism played an important role in undermining authoritarianism and rigidity, but it "too much ignored criteria and defensible standards."

Moral rules and standards are developed in the "responsible interplay of knowledge about human situations and what I would call moral sensitivity," says Sellars. This "would find expression in good reasons," he adds. "Commands need justification." The way of life we seek to evaluate must be thought of in terms of social experimentation and in reflection. Appraisals operate, and "improvement is of the nature of 'better than's'." Sellars continues: "If we have ends-in-view, we seek to appraise their role in our lives in comparison with other ends in the light of the consequences and the satisfactions and dissatisfactions we anticipate. There is interaction between these two kinds of tests [the rational and the functionally empirical] and a playback to the self to make up its mind."[28] In morality, "feeling is operative in a setting of judgment." The "role of the end in one's life economy is envisaged as a result of the interplay of knowledge and feeling. I am not a mere creature of impulse and passions but one who has learned to stop, look and listen." What I want to emphasize are "degrees of adequacy in moral rules and norms," and the possibility, through reflection and conscious effort, based on the findings of experience, of greater adequacy in both rules and norms.

The principles which the rules attempt to articulate are the philosophical ethicist's preeminent concern. There are two poles in moral exploration: the causal and the evaluative. "The social sciences tend to stress the causal. Philosophy must add the evaluative. It must make the effort to clarify ideals and principles . . . It must integrate both means and ends . . . [to determine] what mode of life is desirable and justifiable,"says Sellars. The philosopher indeed has the task of standing back to get perspective on morality and its demands and of undertaking to show which ethical claims are most adequate, and hence defensible. His job is not, therefore, just the disclosure of principles but the determination of the *principle* of moral principles: the meaning and function of morality and its categories, and the how of its most effective formulation.

CHAPTER 6

Humanistic Naturalism in Religion

WHAT, if anything, has reformed materialism to offer in religion? Professor Sellars has written extensively on religion, not always on the basis of reformed materialism, yet always on the basis of a cultural naturalism. Religion he found to be a function of the precariousness of the human situation,[1] with its diverse forms as expressions of diverse types of culture. Historical religions are prescientific and mythological in their explanations. But religion itself is concerned with man's life, in view of the far-flung nature of things.[2] It is therefore a natural and exceedingly important ingredient of human existence — despite its unnaturalistic forms.[3] It is man's sense of cosmic citizenship in the light of his informed or uninformed thinking about the order of things.

Sellars' cultural approach to religion emerged in his studies of Semitics under Craig at Michigan (1902-03) and of Arabic under MacDonald at Hartford Theological Seminary (1903-04). A year at the University of Wisconsin (1904-05) reinforced his humanist perspective. Coming as he did from a medical humanist's background, a realistically scientific humanism was his natural development. He does state on the first page of his unpublished "Biographical Remarks" that he only "gradually became a realist and evolutionary materialist" and that he "did not arrive at these conclusions quickly and easily, but after much conferring." "I think," he wrote, "that I had the gift of pertinacity."

From the humanistic standpoint, Sellars has been a leader. His *Next Step in Religion* (1918) was a pioneer American work in this field and was rated by the New York critic, James G. Hunecker, as one of the two most notable books of that year. (Conrad's *Arrow of Gold* was the other.) And the reviewer in the *Old Orchard News* wrote: "Perhaps no bigger book in point of view of usefulness to the human race has appeared in many moons than *The Next Step in Religion*. It will be welcomed by those interested in human enlightenment as a veritable beacon on the path of progress."

In 1928 Sellars published *Religion Coming of Age* and was soon afterwards selected to draft the Humanist Manifesto. Published in the *New Humanist* (1933), the Manifesto was signed by some thirty humanists. Sellars both preceded and followed the publication of the Manifesto with a number of brief articles in clarification of humanism as a religion. Then, in the 1940's, he was invited to contribute chapters to *Religious Liberals Reply* and *Religion in the Twentieth Century*. The outcome was two papers: "Accept the Universe as a Going Concern" (1947) and "Naturalistic Humanism" (1948). A significant addition to these writings came in the late 1960's in a chapter on "Religious Existentialism" in *Reflections on American Philosophy from Within*.[4] Other unpublished papers have been compiled by Professor Sellars himself for a final rounding out of his thought.

It is not germane to attempt to trace the development of Sellars' thought in the field of religion as we have done in epistemology and ontology; stages do not stand out so clearly. There is, of course, development from a more rhetorical and confident scientific humanism to a more sober, personally and socially problematic humanism, and religion gains in depth and richness with the maturing effects of events over five to six decades.

His first book in the philosophy of religion, *The Next Step in Religion*, was epochal. Combining the findings of anthropological investigation with scientific thought generally, Sellars traced the origins of religions in prescientific thinking and the consequences of this relationship for its literal truth and guidance value. It is not religion, however, which is at fault, but its prescientific orientation. Sellars points out that we live in an utterly different thought - world today from that of the originators of the historical faiths. Religion needs complete reorientation in terms of the vast, precise knowledge of today.

"Having explored the universe by telescope and microscope," Sellars writes, "and having thus come to some understanding of his world, man must return again to his own pressing problems and possibilities. . . . His own life as a realm of affection and action, must rightly be for him the significant center of the universe. These urgencies, interests, possibilities, satisfactions, loyalties, [values] are inalienably human and valid. . . . In his tenser moments, the physical spaces around his planet will but contain 'the endless, silly merriment of the stars.' "

Sellars continues, "As religion learns to relinquish theology and accept the modern view of the world, the spirituality it has fostered will mate with reason,"[5] and reason and feeling will combine in the selection of and commitment to true values.

Here was a philosophy of religion for the sober surviviors of the First World War. A new view of the universe had been forming in their minds, just as it was forming in the minds of other scientific and realistic philosophers. Sellars outlines the latter development in the opening chapter of his volume. In contrast to the dated ideal world of Platonism and the world of form, stuff, and entelechies in Aristotelian thought; in contrast to the three-decker world of the Middle Ages and even its modification in the heavenly city of the eighteenth-century philosophers; in contrast to the mythopoetic thinking of the past, Sellars posits that a "new view of the universe and man's place in it is forming. It is forming in the laboratories of scientists, the studies of thinkers, the congresses of social workers, the assemblies of reformers, the studies of artists and, even more quietly, in the circles of many homes. This new view is growing beneath the old as a bud grows beneath its covering, and is slowly pushing it aside. . . . Mankind grows away from its traditional beliefs as inevitably as does the boy or girl from childhood fancies, and often with the same lack of realization."[6] This lack of realization, however, may extend to the retaining of two disparate views of existence and its functions, each view operational on its own separate occasions. Hence the casting off of the bud's covering may not occur in this century in the religion of many.

We have mentioned that Sellars was more optimistic in his earlier than in his later writing. Not that the universe had changed basically for him, but man and his possibilities have shown a depth of unreason and of impersonally organized social momentum that subtracts from the confidence that "nothing can rob him of the values which he has created."[7] The human situation now looms much more problematic since man himself has "a finger in the pie" and he can do the robbing of his own values. The elements go deeper indeed than the intelligence and will of individual men. Yet the solution is not basically different. For Sellars, it is still that of informed understanding and governance by adequate, precise knowledge:

The new view of the universe is founded upon, influenced by, and has for its necessary setting the exact knowledge which the various special sciences, mental as well as physical, have been accumulating. . . . Incomplete in

> detail though this knowledge may be, man is no longer in the dark as to the main features of his world and his own origin and destiny. He knows that he is an inhabitant of a small planet in one of the many solar systems of the stellar universe, that he is the product of age-long evolution in which variation and survival have been the chief methods of advance, that his mind as well as his body has its natural ancestry. While it will always remain a wonder, so to speak, that there is a universe in which and to which we awaken, it is equally certain that the only sensible thing to do is to seek to find out its character and laws.[8]

Why? Simply to find a basis for living as adequately as possible in terms of their requirements.

This new view of the universe involves both an enlarged conception of the natural order and a redefining of the spiritual. The new naturalism has indeed added a social and spiritual dimension to the biological orientation of the nineteenth century. Man is still an animal, but he is a special development among animals, an animal the content of whose life is molded to an astonishing degree by what has been done in the past by the social groups into which he is born. Culture and civilization are terms essential to his understanding. The gamut of values from the instrumentally physical to fine, lofty, and noble ideals are his natural options. And these options — if relevant — give concreteness to the term "spiritual." The natural therefore encompasses the spiritual.

The term "spiritual" thus also needs redefining. It is a term for all the activities associated with the fine, the beautiful, the good, the right, the noblest, the best, the profoundest. According to Sellars, "The spiritual emerges when there is intelligence of a fairly high order, a sense of right and wrong, an ability to set up standards, a drive for creation in art and social relations, a wealth of imagination,"[9] and a sensitivity in discriminating feelings. That is spiritual which appears to man as significant: "The spiritual is man at his best . . . loving, daring, creating, fighting loyally and courageously for causes dear to him."[10]

Religion and the spiritual are not co-extensive. Religion has a broader and fuller perspective. It is an expression of the human spirit which reflects a cosmic perspective and its objects. And "the breath of the time spirit is always blowing upon it,"[11] the sense of something to be achieved or of something which has been missed. "A man's religion will be his imaginative realization of life." Religion is thus "something larger and more significant than we have been told it was."[12] It does not discount the values of this world and this life. It is loyalty to the real values of this life.

Naturalistic humanism is not negative, denying Christian or Jewish values. It finds continuity in religious developments from prehumanistic spiritualism to naturalistic humanism, and it seeks to develop for man a positive perspective within the framework of a mature type of naturalism, capable of doing justice to the actualities of human life. Sellars describes it as an attempt at the reorientation of religion "in terms of our actual, new knowledge of the nature of the world and the things in it" and our "need to possess a working complex of attitudes, sentiments, and ideas about the meaning of life, the human situation, the kind of universe man is in, and the ideals he should embrace."[13]

Naturalistic humanism has different emphases in different countries, but basically, — yet inclusively, — it is capable of statement in fifteen theses: First, naturalistically religious humanists regard the universe as self-creating and not created. To bring in a supremely intelligent omnipotent power to account for the origin and development of the world is to assume what Hume would have called the greater miracle. Instead of the multiform natural system with its wasteful infinite diversity and blind alleys, one would have to account for a Perfect Being. 'Who made God?' is thus much more than a simple childish question. The universe indeed shows no evidence of being deiform: there is "no logical need for a First Cause if we take the universe to be eternal, much as theists take God to be."[14]

Thesis No. 2 asserts that man is part of nature and that he has emerged as the result of a continuous process. Not only has his body evolved; his mind is quite evidently a function of his brain within his complex organism. It is therefore most intelligible in the light of the amazing story of evolution with its marvelous outcome in terms of capacities and possibilities — including those of moral living, of sensitive satisfactions, and of a sense of cosmic function in a universe terrific in complexity and range.

The third thesis holds that an organic view of life and mind involves the rejection of any dualistic view of mind and body. We have already dealt with this in Chapter 4. Dualism involves an inexplicable nonfunctional fission which does not account for the mind-body harmony that obtains. Nor is the Aristotelian variety of dualism with its distinction of form from prime matter a better formulation than that of the Platonic-Cartesian variety. It is, if anything, more artificial, and likewise leaves unsolved the problem (or problems) of the natural unity of body and mind. In terms of modern science, *mind* is a term for certain integrative activities or operations of the brain. Mind is thus increasingly conceived in adverbial terms, as a qualification of certain neural activities.

The chief implication of this metaphysical monism is that of the non-immortality of the soul or mind. But immortality is no essential of religion. Far Eastern religions place much less stress on immortality than does that mode of Christianity which conceives of salvation in terms of a life after physical death. And immortality is surely no necessary ground for the most meaningful life. Great causes and great values — pearls of great price — are found here and now in living. (To live for the Beyond, at the expense of this life, is scarcely moral religion.)

The fourth thesis of humanism recognizes that man's religious culture and civilization, as depicted by anthropology and history, are the product of a gradual development due to man's interaction with his natural environment and his social heritage. The individual born into a particular culture is molded by that culture. This is certainly more evident in certain faiths than in others. As John F. Kennedy indicated regarding his Catholic faith, he could not help that accident of birth. Even the most open-ended faiths likewise instill their open-endedness, their more free-wheeling convictions and procedures.

The fifth thesis affirms that the nature of the universe depicted by modern science makes unnecessary and unacceptable any supernatural or cosmic guarantees of human values. Humanism does not deny the possibility of realities as yet undiscovered, but it does insist that the way to determine the existence and value of any and all realities is by means of intelligent inquiry and by the assessment of their relation to human needs. Religion must formulate its hopes and plans in the light of the rigors of the scientific spirit and method.

The sixth thesis declares, in the light of the preceding theses, that the time has passed for theism, deism, modernism and the sundry varieties of "new thought." Nature appears self-sufficient and self-conserving, yet shows no evidence of "being replete with purpose and plan."[15]

Thesis No. 7 asserts that religion consists of those actions, purposes and experiences which are humanly significant. Nothing human is alien to it: labor, art, science, philosophy, love, friendship, recreation. It is interesting that Josiah Royce found instances of that loyalty which he took to be preeminently religious in the devotion to duty of a lighthouse keeper, a great military general, and more than one great scientist. "The distinction between the sacred and the secular can no longer be maintained," says Sellars.[16]

The eighth thesis asserts that religious humanism considers the complete realization of the human personality to be the end of human life and seeks its development and fulfillment in the here and now. This is the solution and the explanation of the humanist's social passion.

Thesis Nine maintains that in place of the old attitudes involved in worship and prayer, the humanist finds his emotions expressed in a heightened sense of personal life and in cooperative effort to promote social well-being.

It follows, in Thesis Ten, that there will be no uniquely religious emotion of the kind hitherto associated with belief in the supernatural. The holiness of the "numinous" is, accordingly, not essential to religion; we are indeed more truly religious without it. In place of deference to a *mysterium tremendum,* religious worship will become "at most, cosmic emotion, an almost aesthetic sense of what Santayana calls piety toward the sources of our being. Yet this is scarcely sacred worship."

It may be, however, that the social ritual will evolve with the new setting and its different horizon. A richer and less competitive culture might well find the need to express itself dramatically and artistically. Indeed there is one object toward which a humanist may have an attitude of virtually supreme deference: the integrity of personality and its most adequate fulfillment. A science of intelligent deference could be built around the values of personality and their social conditions. Paramount regard for personalities (note the plural) and their fulfillment is a very different matter from, say, Schweitzer's indiscriminate reverence for life.

The last five theses concern the social and institutional aspects of humanism. We shall simply repeat them from the Manifesto:

"*Eleventh:* Man will learn to face the crises of life in terms of his knowledge of their naturalness and probability. Reasonable and manly attitudes will be fostered and supported by custom. We assume that humanism will take the path of social and mental hygiene and discourage sentimental and unreal hopes and wishful thinking.

"*Twelfth:* Believing that religion must work increasingly for joy in living, religious humanists aim to foster the creative in man and to encourage achievements that add to the satisfactions of life.

"*Thirteenth:* Religious humanism maintains that all associations and institutions exist for the fulfillment of human life. The intelligent evaluation, transformation, control, and direction of such associations and institutions with a view to the enhancement of human life is the purpose and program of humanism. Certainly religious institutions, their ritualistic forms, ecclesiastical methods, and communal activities must be reconstituted as rapidly as experience allows, in order to function effectively in the modern world.

"*Fourteenth:* The humanists are firmly convinced that existing acquisitive and profit-motivated society has shown itself to be inadequate and that a radical change in methods, controls and motives must be instituted. A socialized and cooperative economic order must be established to the end that the equitable distribution of the means of life be possible. The goal of humanism is a free and universal society in which people voluntarily and intelligently cooperate for the common good. Humanists demand a shared life in a shared world. [In *The Humanist* for January/February 1973, Corliss Lamont would like to see this fourteenth thesis eliminated. And in view of the development in Sellars' social philosophy, discussed in the next chapter, there is no doubt that he would now significantly modify his statement of this point].

"*Fifteenth and last:* We assert that humanism will: (a) affirm life rather than deny it; (b) seek to elicit the possibilities of life, not flee from it; and (c) endeavor to establish the conditions of a satisfactory life for all, not merely for the few. By this positive *morale* and intention humanism will be guided, and from this perspective and alignment the techniques and efforts of humanism will flow."[17]

We have now given the framework of religious humanism. It remains to give more of its actual flesh and blood and to disclose its vital dimensions. We have said that Sellars' humanism is not negative. It can include any positive components of religion which can be certified in terms of authenticity. But we have to watch the word "authentic" since it is used in special senses that have meaning only to those who are specifically informed. Our own usage calls for disciplined thought and critical experience, but not for a special process that could be characterized as initiation.

We shall both amplify and appraise Sellars' humanism in terms of the religious dimensions it offers in comparison with those of other faiths, and we shall begin with its horizontal scope or breadth. What range of perspective does it offer to man? And how relevantly? Religion, states Sellars, is living in view of the far-flung nature of things in a universe marvelous in complexity and range. It is no mere urban or local citizenship which it bespeaks, but because one needs some understanding of himself and the kind of world he is in, a cosmic perspective and piety can and should suffuse man's overall activities and relations. His work and play, art and business, and organizational participations whatever their nature, may all therefore be religious.

"Yes," says Sellars, "man is in nature. Nature is his home and area of life and of competence. Let the artist and poet speak out here. Even music and language are inseparable from vibrations. And yet man is himself — not a *part* merely, but an agent, dreamer, chooser, and thinker. Let the existentialism of Kierkegaard be enlarged and made realistic. Aesthetics and ethics? Yes. Religion? Yes. But let it be a religion which courageously looks this-ward at man's inescapable task and opportunity. . . . A cosmic view and a planetary view, a social view and an intrinsically personal view. These must be woven into a well-evidenced and constantly tested perspective. So runs the manifesto of humanism."[18]

The perspective is inclusive of all that is well-evidenced. Even Kierkegaard's type of supernaturalism is intelligible in terms of the psychology of its assumptions and the sociology of its conditions though it is not defensible in its wishful, dogmatic claims. Kierkegaard had too few alternatives before him. But this matter involves another dimension: the historical time dimension. We might be tempted to think of this as religion's dimension of length, but time is infinitely more than duration. It is a relation of events in their fullness and depth: the flow of multitudinous interwoven influences from one state of affairs to another. The making of a Confucian or Buddhist culture is an example of the time dimension in religion; the experiences of the Hebrews in the wilderness is a more specific example; the prophets drawing inferences from the events that beset their people is still more definitive.

Religion looks both forwards and backwards: to its goals and to its sources. It is a time-conscious aspect of man's living, putting an emphasis on the action or process. Even the qualitative Johannine injunction that this is life eternal that they may know the true God, is an injunction toward what D. C. Macintosh called a religious adjustment. The religious use of the favorite term "eternity" has often put it in opposition to events in time as though eternity could be abstracted from happenings that constitute it any more than existence can be abstracted from things that exist. Yet the latter is a fallacy to which certain existentialists are peculiarly liable.

There is a tension, to be sure, between religious strands which emphasize works and those trends which put their preeminent stress upon faith. It will be recalled that Martin Luther called the epistle of James "a right strawy epistle." Yet even the exercise of faith involves events in time, with antecedents and consequences for the sake of some mode of eternal life. There is thus a time-consciousness at the very heart of religion.

Now time-consciousness is something that Sellarsian humanists clearly stress. The breath of the time spirit, we have said, is always blowing on the activities we call spiritual.[19] Man himself indeed has emerged as the result of a continuous process. Character and culture are both resultants of gradual processes. Religion consists of those actions, purposes, and experiences that are humanly significant. The realization of human personality is the indirect goal of human life, while cooperative effort to achieve social well-being is a more direct objective. Humanism affirms life itself rather than denies it, seeking to elicit the possibilities in life, and endeavoring to establish the conditions of a satisfactory life for all.

There is, to be sure, a narrower use of the term *eternal*, in the sense of enduring verities. That which endures throughout different ages and diverse social conditions we may think of as eternal. In thinking of familiar realities, however, our perspective is likely to be limited to such a period as that of human civilization. We find that the hills which endure, for example, have not by any means always existed. So this is a usage which is open to question. But humanism no less than Pauline Christianity puts an emphasis on enduring values. Whatsoever things are true and of good report will continue to be valid values for humans under very many circumstances. No continuous realization of personality or of social well-being is possible without them.

But this leads us to the third dimension of religion: its height. Historically, religions divide into nature religions and ethical religions. There is a sense of height in nature religions, symbolized in Greek thought by Mount Olympus. It is a height of special privilege and power. We shall ignore this kind of religious elevation. The ethical religions not only feature moral codes but they tend toward, if not culminate in, a perfectionist ethic. "Be ye perfect therefore as your father in heaven is perfect," is translated in the Sermon on the Mount, as "Don't have any but the purest motives." This may involve "an inexperience of faith," which as T. V. Smith wrote, "may either tear down or build up, a world."[20]

From the humanist standpoint religion concerns values: the importances of things of any and all kinds for human beings. It is loyalty to the real values of life and concern for their perpetuation. The spiritual, we have quoted, is "man at his best . . . loving, daring, creating, fighting loyally and courageously for causes dear to him."[21] His sense of importances is therefore keen and strong.

Distinction of importances involves standards, with shades of goodness and badness, rightness and wrongness. Morality is not necessarily religious in the traditional sense of the religious. But as discrimination of what comprises good living in the kind of world we are in, morality is religious, and humanism as a religion is most notably a moral religion.

It is not, however, simply concerned with moral values. It espouses all types of values: aesthetic, recreational, purely personal, and ideal. Ideal values are not just the prerogative of otherworldly perfectionists. Religious humanism, for example, considers "the complete realization of the human personality to be the end of man's life." But this is an ideal which is never attained: it is an ongoing process which is always incomplete. There is a difference, however, between perfect ideals of the supernaturalists and the ideals of humanists. Ideals for the latter are formed in terms of relevantly informed possibilities for progressive achievement with no all-at-once assumptions. They may be perfectionist in an essentially realistic, here-and-now relevant sense. They are not perfectionist in the sense of denying or ignoring steps and stages of attainment. Humanistic ideals are thus informative and directive ideals.

"All the ontological categories apply to man," declares Sellars. "He is a creature of time, space, and substance. And yet within this immense and inescapable framework man has his unique and specialized capacities and endeavors. He is not only a knower but also an agent and an eager desirer of good things."[22] He is capable of both height and depth in life.

We are therefore distinguishing depth from man's aspirations and ideals. Depth, as Sellars states, is of course a metaphor as were our terms for the other dimensions, but depth has been made much of in depth psychology, depth theology, etc. Depth psychology has emphasized feeling and drive in opposition to mere intellectualism, but it too has called for intellectualization. "Depth theology and *encounter* claims seems to me to belong to a different gambit, that of mysticism. The idea is that one can dig down to God and the supernatural," says Sellars.[23] But one had better examine his presuppositions and processes of inquiry. Depth ultimately concerns foundations; if these cannot be intelligently clarified, their claims are dogmatic or simply wishful espousals.

Sellars has, interestingly, dealt with Tillich and others from this standpoint. In the interests of succinctness, we shall use his treatment of Tillich in *Reflections on American Philosophy From Within*. Tillich represents the theological crosscurrents sufficiently to be a good example of the attempt to update theology in terms of its historical traditions. In his estimation of Tillich, Sellars says that "the matrix of Tillich's philosophy, if I judge correctly, is a fusion of Kantianism, Platonism and German idealism with undertones of Husserlian phenomenology. This is a heady mixture, especially when it is suffused with theological motivations. Through it shines a very honest and enlightened personality. But is it valid?"[24]

Sellars comments: "On Page 334 of the *Theology of Paul Tillich*, he asserts that 'the unsymbolic statement which implies the necessity of religious symbolism is that God is being itself, and as such is beyond the subject-object structure of everything that is.' Here we find in a nutshell the foundation of his ontology and his apparently daring assertions that God does not exist, that He is beyond existence. He is the abyss, the Ground. God is not a being among other beings."[25] Shades of Plotinus!

For Sellars, it is crucial to know, "How does Tillich get to Being itself, this Ground or Abyss, to which all symbols are tied. . . . As nearly as I can make out he moves to it along Platonic and Aristotelian lines . . . I think that Professor Randall is right in treating Tillich as belonging to Augustinian tradition as enlarged by German idealism . . . Tillich began with a theistic theology and fitted his epistemology into it. . . . What is primary, then, for a knowledge terminating in basic ontology is a kind of participation in true being, a participation which unites love with cognition. But this kind of cognition seems to work largely in terms of symbols elicited by encounters. This gives what Tillich calls a 'belief-ful or self-transcending realism.' " But encounters with what? Studies of the sense of parental presence among children are revealing. "A child develops expectations with regard to its mother and tends to see her at any signal."[26] Was it Carl Erskine who talked companionably to God on the pitching mound? Theological conditioning and self-hypnosis are quite possible to people who in Platonic-Kantian fashion separate being from things that exist. Says Sellars: "I take his Being itself as an echo of Kant's noumenal world beyond phenomenal existence." This is accompanied by "a tendency to put assigned significance above historical fact."[27] The consistent upshot of this would be a treatment of nature in symbolic rather than realistic terms, though Tillich valued the sciences and art too highly to go to quite such lengths.

"What then I am calling attention to," Sellars explains, "is that Tillich makes his precarious leap of faith to Being Itself in the setting of philosophical traditions very much alive in the Germany of his time, but being challenged in the United States of my era."[28] Tillich's leap to Being Itself is the importation into America of a movement growing out of the neo-orthodoxy of the postwar period. To give a raison d'être to Being Itself apart from existing things, Tillich inflates being "in terms of what he calls 'depth of reason' and an ontological reason which grasps and shapes reality to attain an approach to an objective Logos, all of which savors of romantic idealism."[29] It has no public experimental basis; Tillich turns his back on an orientation which stresses evidence and proceeds to inflate a supersensible reality.

Tillich himself acknowledges the mythology of much theological thinking but then proceeds to fashion his own theological fairyland. But we need a religion for this world of our practical as well as theoretic activity, and we need to see these two types of activity interplaying with each other. Surely our socio-cultural problems are expressions of our workaday conditions, and it is in facing up to realities of things and events as they confront us in effective living that we find the direct province of religion. To divert ourselves from immediate issues to a supersensible world is to prepare ourselves badly for any world.

Tillich had at best too great a hiatus between the world of things and events and the world of ultimate concern, and his connections are basically imaginative — with no demonstrated foundations. "What I offer in naturalistic humanism," says Sellars, "is an outlook which works within the world, stressing explanation and creative mastery . . . I would . . . stress . . . the quality of life and . . . new levels."[30] What Tillich calls a sense of dependence, Sellars calls a sense of realities. But a sense of realities does not preclude aspiration and rational enthusiasism, says Sellars: "A certain wonderment, indeed, a standing back and looking at nature and life should be encouraged. It might even take the interrogative form of why is there anything, and not merely 'nothingness'."[31] Why is there so very much? But such interrogations should be governed by disciplined and informed thought if one's query is one of real concern. Imaginative speculations are entertaining and suggestive, but under what circumstances are they really relevant and valid? When are they based on demonstrable foundations?

Professor Marten Ten Hoor has queried whether Sellars has really done justice to the phenomena of religion represented by the more intensive supernaturalists.[32] I have already quoted Sellars regarding the assimilability of Kierkegaard. Let the latter be enlarged and made realistic and he becomes assimilable. His intellectual and social conditions can be understood, as indeed can his type of anti-intellectualism. It is an emphasis on factual intelligibility which characterizes Sellars' intellectualism; Sellars can assimilate Freudianism with its anti-intellectualism but with its stress on the importance of understanding the anti-intellectual dynamisms and their products. A patient is thereby on the way to mental health. Similarly with the people who find a respite from unpleasant realities in otherwordly faiths and the rites which accompany such major occasions as marriage and death: understanding the dynamisms and their products is essential here also. The recourse to mystery, to transempirical solvents, to piety, to a Messiah coming on the cloud of heaven, or to a Neoplatonic or, alternatively, Aristotelian cosmos, or a Kantian noumenal realm — these are devices by which humans have tried to cope with their sense of predicament. Sellars' religion, contrarily, is realistically profound and challenging. There is scant escapism in it. It is the tough-minded, scientifically oriented person indeed who cannot accept the dated Platonisms and Kantianisms, or see the possibility of actually updating Aristotle; it is the realistically tough-minded who can accept the universe as a going concern, and make the most of life in these realistic terms. More and more of life is being governed by the realities disclosed by the sciences, and the province left free for supernaturalistic over-beliefs is decreasing. Sellars' faith is thus at least directional. It is a faith for the future and it is indeed increasing as a faith of the present for consistently honest minds.

CHAPTER 7

Projective Social Realism[1]

IT IS not uncommon to conclude the account of a person's philosophy with a statement of his intellectual position in religion. Religion adds a large cosmic dimension to life. It is, we have seen for Sellars, man's living "in view of the far-flung nature of things." But the category of the social for Sellars is men's living together in view of everything. It is therefore, in Dewey's words and Sellars' thought, an "inclusive category." It is especially appropriate, therefore, to conclude our treatment of Roy Wood Sellars with his social philosophy. This was an intense interest of his. Even in ethics his concern was preeminently institutional.

It is not surprising, therefore, to find him writing in 1949: "It will, I believe, interest my readers to find a materialist recognizing the normative as a guiding factor in the moral order intrinsic to group life . . . surely, group life and with it, the socialized human being lifted to the level of humanity thereby, involves a moral order. The thing to do is to make it explicit. . . . But this does not mean that they (moral principles) are non-natural, for man is, in group life, a moral being."[2]

Sellars' social concern began, we have noted in Chapter 1, while he was a student at the Ferris Institute in 1897-98. There he selectively read Bellamy, Morris, and Ball, and became skeptical of statesmen as prisoners of their respective social systems. His social concern took *public* form while he was an undergraduate. In 1902 he published in the University of Michigan *Inlander* a substantial article on the "Re-interpretation of Democracy" as it was developing in American life. And in 1916 — the same year that Rand McNally published his *Critical Realism* — the Macmillan Company issued his *Next Step in Democracy*. A really moral, gradualistic socialism was the next step. He had minored in sociology with Charles Horton Cooley for his doctorate, and he had assimilated at the University of

Wisconsin some of the progressivism in that state's climate of opinion. LaFollette was the outstanding political figure in Wisconsin at the time. It was to be expected, therefore, that he should begin teaching social philosophy at a relatively early stage — 1914 seems to have been the first year — and that he should build his course as an evaluation or critique of the several socialist movements. He distinguished three stages of socialism: Utopian socialism; Marxist socialism; and a gradualistic, Fabian kind of socialism. The third type was envisaged as the clearly developmental and realistic kind of socialism.

But Sellars' social philosophy is not simply to be categorized as socialistic. It had too many dimensions for so simple a label. We must grasp its groundwork and outreach. I quote my own 1970 summation: "Teaching social philosophy some 34 years and beginning historically with the political thought and textures of the Greek city states — while engaged in a critical examination of socialism as a philosophy — Sellars traced socio-political formulations through Plato, Aristotle, Roman political idealogy, Christian medievalism, Machiavelli, Hobbes, Locke, Rousseau, early collectivism, Marx, dialectical and historical materialism, Russian applications and deviations, ideological democracy, fascism and national socialism to current issues and trends."[3]

According to Sellars: "Social philosophy grew out of ideology somewhat as chemistry grew out of alchemy. The word 'ideology' has had, of course, as loose a set of meanings as any astrologer might want: from vague slogan-type polarizations in social sentiments and unscientific mystical abstractions that may or may not be social, to any intellectualizing of the social life of man. In general, however, ideologies have polarized both the social thought and social emotions of man. Ideologies are 'to be regarded as preliminary attempts at social and political philosophy or at least gestures in that direction. [Yet] often they are not more than hasty generalizations."[4]

Sellars early distinguished three approaches which can be made to the problems of social philosophy and the evaluation of ideological systems. He called the first one the "approach from beneath." It is that of a behavioristic objectivism, emphasizing inventions, patterns of action, facts. Secondly, he discriminated an "approach from within." Here behavior deepens into linguistic behavior which has two interacting dimensions, the personal and social, reflection and communication. Here we are brought to cultural history and its great ages.[5] Ideologies are important for this approach. Institutions are expressions of patterns of thought that, in turn, express patterns of value.

The third approach has more psychological balance and philosophical distance:

> [It] sought, in the social sciences and philosophy, to stand back and appraise as validly as possible, criteria and directions . . . a sort of meta-affair. . . . In it one must have balance and breadth of outlook. I have acknowledged that, during the years I have maintained my dialogue on social questions, there have been great advances in the social sciences. Yet there have been certain hesitancies in regard to framework. Is behaviorism adequate? Or must we somehow fit in values? And what in hell are values? [The issue of values and standards of value is indeed fundamental to this approach.]
>
> I shall now break loose and offer what the Germans call a Weltanschauung, which can be designated, as per wish, an ideology, perspective or outlook. As I see it, these approaches converge on some such stance, decision or commitment. And here I speak . . . in my . . . role as a philosopher. . . . I am not, to use A. J. Ayer's term, a pontiff in philosophy nor pontifically inclined. Nor do I quite like his alternative phrase, 'journeyman.' I always thought of myself as facing up to genuine problems upon which, no doubt, science had been working but which were not explicitly on its agenda, such as the nature of perceiving and the reach and status of the knowledge claims which developed within it, the correct formulation of the mind-body problem and the status of mental activity as causally guiding behavior.
>
> Here I worked along the line of signals, the role of information, the solving of adjustmental problems and what I called an emergent level of causality. In short, I was not an epiphenomenalist of the Huxley type. I had a high respect for the ingenuity of nature and for its anagenetic resources. All this led me to a double-knowledge approach to the mind-brain situation and, as an empiricist, I was persuaded that in awareness we had an operation essential to this level of causal activity. In short, I had become a critical realist, an emergent evolutionist, and a reformed materialist. These, if you will, are my philosophical isms. I think they will have bearing on social philosophy in a not too peripheral way.
>
> I have defined man as not only an historical animal but as a metaphysical one. And here I use this latter term in the setting of an emergent, or reformed, materialism rather than in that of existentialism. I make no play on nothingness and death. Man is recognizedly mortal, yet is able to 'look before and after and sigh for what is not.' He has his frustrations, alienations and estrangements, even in an affluent society. He is a metaphysical animal in that he wants to know his place in the universe and what meanings he can

give to his life. I would put reasoned recognition above religious myths. . . . On what can we build? And what is socially possible and desirable? These questions play back into social philosophy. I think the reader can see why I conceive of it as a responsible dialogue.[6]

It is a dialogue singularly alert to realities. Socio-moral principles may indeed vary from culture to culture and yet be concerned with roles of people and things in the lives of men. Such principles, Sellars has emphasized, are fundamental to the social life of people. They are disclosed by informed discussion of social processes. The function of the physical, together with all basic and higher values, must be envisaged in the principles of good social life.

The role of rationality in Sellars' social philosophy is given special focus in a 1943 article entitled "Reason and Revolution." Opposition to World War II had been leading some to call and work for revolution. But is revolution the only alternative? "To be emotionally against an unpleasant event is surely not enough . . . ," Sellars observes. "Reason tells us that it is necessary to set forces to work designed to weaken and counteract those factors tending to bring unpleasant and destructive events to pass."[7] The article concludes with a statement based on Aristotle's analysis of kinds of government and their relevance to the causes of revolution. All governments are faulty when tried by an adequate rather than purely relative standard, Sellars says:

Is it presumptuous of me to suggest that democracy has not yet passed from the stage of ideology and shibboleth to that maturer level of assured principle and commitment at which Aristotle hints? May not a social philosophy of such a kind, if found and adopted, be the best preservative of democracy? If might can ever be harnessed to the chariot of right, it must be tamed and subdued by a reason which has found sponsors in the varied life of mankind.[8]

Based on recognition of conjoint behavior and the interrelations of people in groups, Sellars' social philosophy is a true social realism. And it is not a static social realism. It is characterized indeed by three dimensions: (1) historical background and perspective — we have already demonstrated this; (2) sociological depth, pointing to the "different levels of society . . . varying centers and controls" and, presumably, hidden factors in social process; (3) triangulation, pointing up desirable directions on the basis of the findings of the great social thinkers (and the points of their directional intersections): Plato, Hobbes, Locke, Jefferson, Marx. As Sellars says:

History no doubt gives a sense of depth but only if it has a cumulative dimension. It must be supplemented by sociology . . . in depth — even a biological perspective is needed to help free us from . . . naïve teleology or purposiveness in things.

Among other things, in the world today, capitalism and communism confront one another. As ideologies, they snarl at each other; but philosophy and sociology must look at them in depth and then it is seen that they have much in common. Both are to be justified only by what they accomplish in the way of a satisfying human life. . . .

To get perspective one must add comparative studies to history and these must be given the backgrounds of political geography and economic geography. Only after all this has been done has one a sense of depth, of dimension.[9]

How, now, to pinpoint Sellars' social philosophy more specifically? I shall use the figure of a continental explorer to make Sellars' intellectual findings more vivid. In Sellars' philosophy throughout, we have been crossing a number of historically philosophical divides: the divide between the mind and the body, the divide between the sensations and ideas of the mind and external physical objects (i.e., outside the body), and the divide between the self-conscious agential beings such as we conceive ourselves to be and primeval substance or inorganic matter. Crossing each of the divides took decades in the development of Sellars' thought.

Sellars' social philosophy constitutes his effort to cross a fourth divide: the divide between individualistic wishes and social necessity. This fourth divide is one which many people besides philosophers are deeply concerned to cross. The spectrum of those lined up for this crossing includes all who, like Martin Luther King, have had some kind of a dream of a much better state of affairs. The relevance of epistemology and ontology to contemporary living is brought out by Sellars' social philosophy.

Though he began writing on this issue while still an undergraduate, he kept notably up-to-date. He published in 1970, after his ninetieth birthday, a major study on *Social Patterns and Political Horizons*, and the New Left gets references and paragraphs in his last three or so chapters.

That he has been at grips with this problem throughout his professional life is witnessed by his publication in 1916 — a year before the Russian Revolution — of a treatise on socialism. Marxist communism is dealt with in this volume as the second of three stages of socialism. And in comparison with a society like the American, Marxism is found wanting. Marxism, however, is entitled to its credits: its realistic consciousness of downright social ills, its sense of social process and of the basic importance of physical needs and their adequate meeting, its awareness of the need of a total conception of man and his world. "Nothing human," Marx maintained, "is alien to me."[10] Yet Marx himself has been taken out of context and treated as a distorter of the human situation. Still, I have drawn the inference from Sellars' writing that Marx is certainly as one-sided in his criticism of capitalistic society as his critics are of him.

Marxism is, however, a complex theory, not to be discounted by any simple criterion or limitation. It is a conception of men in society, of a social way of life. Only the comparative method, which juxtaposes the total system to its alternatives — including one's own — can give a fair evaluation. And this evaluation must take account of historical conditions and their comparative development. But it must also meet the tests of reliable knowledge, of documentable cosmology, and of adequate value theory.

Social philosophy can attempt to elaborate in independent terms. Like all other realms of philosophy, social philosophy for Sellars is a *meta* affair, an objective commentary that takes account of findings from all sources: scientific, humanistic, and socially practical. Yet philosophy is commentary that has an adequate theoretical structure and outlook. Framework and perspective are the very heart of philosophy, and it is these that give substance and defensibility to any human endeavor. In Sellars' earlier years, when he was working on the main concepts of modern science, he characterized philosophy as the completion of science. Philosophy undertook to show the basis and structure of the chief categories which scientists use. He could have said the same thing about philosophy and religion when he wrote his two books on religion. Philosophy also completes religion. Until religion has acquired a philosophical orientation, it has no substantiality or consistency of thought.

It is interesting that in his very last book Sellars should say the same thing about Marxist social ideas and practice: "By having a sort of social philosophy Marx succeeded in giving the incipient socialist movement a feeling of emotional and intellectual self-sufficiency. The theoretician had an answer to questions almost in terms of chapter and verse."[11]

The big social problem today, therefore, is by no means solely a practical problem, or even a scientific problem. It is basically a philosophical matter. Sellars wrote that "after philosophy gets through the brambles of technical problems it has inherited it should aim at desirable possibilities in the human scene. It should work with both popular culture, expressive of the new media of communication, and the humanistic tradition in art and literature. Nor should it neglect the work of the behavioral sciences, including cultural anthropology. But, as I said, it should aim at an overall assessment of the human scene."[12] Perspective and framework as already stated, are the heart of philosophy, whether social or impersonal. The basic technical problems are not to be bypassed. And to be adequate to the human scene, philosophy must in its special way aid in the achieving of a harmony of thought and feeling.

We have our not-too-human situation: power-blocks of people juxtaposed to each other; underprivileged and unprivileged peoples both outside and inside these social blocks; established social systems and accepted socioeconomic philosophies wrestling with the problems arising in their respective cultures. We also have social philosophers attempting to be objective about the systems in which they not merely live but must undertake to work, and to be comparative about the systems in which others live and work and the conditions they are attempting to meet. These philosophers bespeak the spearhead of social advance.

"As an internationalist," Professor Sellars wrote, "I would stress a withdrawal from militarism and a gentling of human relations, resting on imaginative fellow-feeling. The problems are real and must be faced.

"The youth may well be somewhat hard on the older generation, but it should also be 'hard' on itself. And the same holds for the older generation. If there is a 'greening of the youth' going on, it should be encouraged to come to flower. There are great possibilities before mankind. But correct assessment and institutional change will not be easy."[13]

I want on this basis to juxtapose Sellars to two prominent social philosophers: Herbert Marcuse and John Dewey.

Dewey's social concern stands out in his life and philosophy. He went back to the time of Henry George and Edward Bellamy. At one time he announced that he would edit a journal of social criticism and constructive social programming. But he was dissuaded from this by attacks from the Detroit press. Yet his preeminent concern continued to be with social problems. Stephen Pepper treats his prime contribution to ethics as the discovery and elaboration of the social context theory, and certainly this comes closer to accounting for the development of morality than does a personal context theory.

But overlapping contexts present a problem for this theory, though they set the stage for a more general social philosophy. Dewey's emphases on the pervasiveness and inclusiveness of the social factor, i.e., the role of conjoint behavior, marks him as a social realist. The social is one type of reality that is not in question for him. (He has also been classed as a perspectival realist, holding that things are real for the relations in which they obtain. Sidney Hook has likewise shown that he is very minimally a metaphysical realist upholding a general metaphysics of instruments as such. These other realisms, however, are open to serious questions: the second because of its gross incompleteness; the first for its naïve inability to distinguish the objects of normal from abnormal perception.)

Dewey's social realism, together with his stress on problem-solving, is his actual forte. And socially, who does not know that we need problem-solving in far-reaching ways? The question is: Does Dewey have a sufficient basis for problem-solving, social or non-social? A purely contextual problem-solving is not enough; contexts overlap. We need to know what kind of men have the problems as well as what kind of problems men have, and what kind of world they are in. Apparent solutions to problems can be non-basic. Without detracting anything whatever from John Dewey's impact on the social world or from his actual contribution to philosophy, we can, and ought to, recognize a series of inadequacies: the lack of an actual theory of perceptual knowledge which would enable him to discriminate individuals as such; the lack of an epistemology per se (he deprecated epistemology because of its historical connection with "under the hat," Cartesian-type dualisms); the lack of an adequate ontology (his naturalism was purely methodological, and based on the method of science; there is something phenomenalistic about such a naturalism); and, finally, a lack of an adequate conception of personality. Dewey, of course, had a Vermont American's sense of individuality (and he certainly had a robust individuality of his own.) But this sense is taken for granted rather than provided for in this theory. In *Experience and Nature* he has an indirect argument for individuality from the case for inventiveness and originality. In the same work he makes the notably indefinite statement that "existentially speaking, a human individual is a distinctive opacity of bias and preference conjoined with plasticity and permeability of needs and likings."[14] His very focus on problem-solving treats individuals, whether things or persons, as ingredients of problems to be solved or as subtending relations that comprise the solutions to problems rather than the heart of the solution. He does indeed pinpoint the problems of men as the problems of human concern, but he does so somewhat in the sense that another student of Hegel, Karl Marx, treated men in general and in the mass. The sense of interrelation growing out of Dewey's early, modified Hegelian orientation, provides a tension for his Vermont individualism.

Roy Wood Sellars is, like Dewey, a social realist — so much so, in fact, that in 1916 he considered himself a socialist. Social patterns, institutions, groupings, roles, obligations are elements of a fabric within which man has his being. It was with reference to the lack of recognition of these social components and bonds that Sellars wrote in his undergraduate article that a type of democracy which insisted on separate, rugged individualities, on a negative rather than mutually participative democracy "ended by losing, partially at least, any but the external bonds of union. Social forces were curbed by the non-social. . . . Yet the extreme of rabid individualism . . . gradually defeated itself. Of late years in consequence the American people have recognized the social side of life and laid stress on the responsibility of all citizens to all citizens."[15]

Sellars' social realism is based on the nature and stature of persons. His theory of perceptual knowledge discriminates things and persons, not simply problems or relations. Entities, living or inanimate, exist indeed in situations; it is not the situation which is discriminated, however, but Mr. A in situation X, or Mr. A and colleagues in situation Y, and Mr. A in a series of contexts. This balance between the individual and social with the recognition that individuals are primary in their social context, and that social contexts are contexts of human individualities, and of high importance for individualities — this recognition of the humanly personal meaning of the social is distinctive of Sellars.

This attitude indeed could also be said of certain personal idealists, and yet Sellars is no personal idealist. He surmounted that liability while studying James Ward in his philosophical youth. Sellars, we have pointed out, is a substantive, evolutionary naturalist with an identity theory of the brain-mind relation. His conception of the human brain is that of a minded brain. How than can he have this emphasis on persons?

"It may, to some, appear strange," we quoted Sellars in Chapter 5, "that a materialist should so emphasize the self and call attention to its configurated interests and admirations. . . . But the philosophical materialist is an empiricist, though a realistic one. He sees no reason not to acknowledge the fact that the human, organic self is gifted with the capacity of cognitive reference and appraisal. . . ."[16] And Sellars does see reason, he wrote elsewhere, to recognize a very distinctive level of causality in human life: *the level of agential causality*, which gives to human beings the prerogatives of decision and assumption of undertakings that quite commonly in modern contextual life are, in some sense at least, collaborative ventures. Man therefore assumes responsibilities in society.

Yet having shown the central importance of the individual for a theory of society, we must look at the other side of the issue: the importance of the social fabric for the individual. Here is where Marcuse comes in. The social fabric, for him, is quite completely determinative of the character and quality of personal life. Adopted as the philosophical spokesman of the New Left, Marcuse's key term is *liberation*. The liberation he envisages is the emancipation of man per se from an archaic, uncoordinated process of production which operates with alienated labor. This system must be displaced everywhere, in existing communistic countries as well as capitalistic ones, since the former have become bureaucratic and therefore untrue to Marxist principles. Associated individuals must take over on behalf of freedom and universal human satisfactions. For when these associated persons shall have assumed "the direction of the life-process and have made the totality of social relations the work of reason and their freedom, what man is in himself will be related to his existence in a new way. The formerly contingent and 'inessential' will now represent the fulfillment of the most authentic possibilities. Man will then have to be 'defined' not as a free rational being in opposition to the contingent conditions of life but as the free and rational creator of his conditions of life, as the creator of a better and happier life."[17]

Two of the three sentences seem existentialist. They are certainly sweepingly general enough to satisfy the emotionally toned person. But Marcuse is no existentialist. He is a neo-Marxist who tried to do for Marx somewhat substantially what Berkeley and Hume tried to do for Locke, i.e., to make him self-consistent. The result indeed is comparable. Marxism is construed in basically revolutionary and international terms. Sellars states that Marcuse's outlook seems evolutionary in tone. There are, however, different stages in his writing. In 1937 he seemed more evolutionary than in 1967. I would rather say that Marcuse's philosophy is non-bloody in tone, though he is quite prepared to accept and even to have people provoke bloodshed. The job of the "radical opposition" (which is the term he uses most frequently) is to be ready for, and to assist in bringing about, a break in the capitalistic system, and then to step in with a totally new order of associated individuals. It is not simply the social order in a particular region at a particular time, let me repeat, that is to be displaced; it is existing society everywhere. The radical opposition, Marcuse writes, must be envisaged today, "only in a global framework."[18] A universally new society is therefore to be created in which all needs of everyone will be satisfied. This new society, Marcuse thinks, is no dyslogistical utopia, since we have the knowledge and instrumentalities for meeting every need. It is a matter of application. *But the how of the organization of the new society and the logistics of the total set of operations are not to be discovered in any historical models of society.* There is a real messianism about Marcuse's new order. The biblical statement, that "in that hour it shall be given thee what thou shalt say" and do, seems presupposed. Marcuse, of course, has the Hegelian dialectical logic, as well as Marx's dialectical materialism, to undergird him. But one has to be a believer already to accept these a priori patterns. Both Hegel and Marx are pre-Darwinian in their evolutionary thinking, and Marcuse's willingness at points to discount facticity[19] in the interests of his theory indicates that Darwin must be assimilated to Hegel rather than to the converse. Evolutionary thought has, however, come a long way since Marx and Hegel, yet the fixity of social species which Sellars found characteristic of Marx is evidently just as characteristic of Marcuse. Those members of the New Left who take Marcuse as their philosophical spokesman need to know how dated some of his assumptions are. Some of them need likewise to know what Dean Inge stated so aphoristically: "He who is married to the spirit of his time will soon be a widower."

Sellars, interestingly, has two things in common with Marcuse: (1) the conviction that we should not compromise on social goals; and (2) a belief in the materialistic bases of society. Common to them also, I think, is the corollary that morality is more relevant on a materialistic foundation than its alternatives. since morality in Sellars' words concerns the down-to-earth problems of "human living together." Sellars is also basically sympathetic with the victims of those human ills to which the New Left has been, in its sweeping way, addressing itself. But there the similarity ceases. Sellars' goals are not to be encompassed by a slogan such as liberation; they are more specific. Justice, for example, is not to be equated with equality, though equality is a basic value — the starting point, indeed — for justice. The factors of individual differences must be taken into account by one's principles of justice. They are difficult to provide for on a thesis of simple equality. And goals generally require an elaboration through the mill of experience and historical process.

Sellars' philosophy of history, furthermore, is quite different from Marcuse's. It is not *a priori*. It is scientifically oriented in the fullest sense, yet equally humanistic. Values are the distinguishing features of human existence: the things to enjoy and admire, the things to love, the things to aspire to, the things to assume responsibility for and to strive for. Aesthetic, moral, religious, social, and intellectual values, the whole range of objects which human ascriptions and working appraisals find meaningful in and for the total pattern of life, these are all to be encompassed in a realistic philosophy of man. Sellars' materialism is in no sense reductive.

It is evolutionary and therefore historical in a quasi-experimental sense. "No a priori path is set. In this sense existence precedes essence.' " This marks a significant difference between Sellars and Marcuse. "I take cultural development to have been worked out historically," wrote Sellars. "Man evolved his big brain biologically but his scientific method historically."[20] There is, in Sellars' writing, a sense of social achievement rather than a sense of social failure. The achievement is, accordingly, not lightly to be thrown away. Marcuse too, assuredly, does not want to dispense with industry and technology. These are essential for a "pacified society." But Sellars recognizes historical achievements in democracy within capitalistic systems. Social systems, especially democratically open systems, have a flexibility that neither Marx nor Marcuse recognized. Capitalism in its actual operation is not merely an economic system. It is part of a total cultural pattern. Sellars has argued the same point for Marx's historical materialism. It is a complex cultural matter and by no means purely economic. Similarly democratic capitalistic systems are cultural matters. Capitalism has shown itself flexible within a democratic culture, though its adjustments have tended to be quite belated. It is capable nonetheless of meeting human needs, and of doing so with challenging opportunities. "Challenge" is a term I have seen little of in the writings of Marcuse. The problem with a capitalistic economy is how to secure the humanistic motivations at the heart of the culture and thereby to facilitate the throwing out of challenges that service human needs. *The system itself must adjust to its cultural matrix. And the humanistic character of the matrix must be inculcated in the system.* We must develop a strategy of realistic brotherhood or fraternity which is by its very nature a strategy of peace.

Sellars argues for "a two-way approach in social theory: on the one hand, *an attempt to clarify goals for humanity* — an effort as old as Stoicism, Buddhism, and Christianity . . . taken up again in the Enlightenment . . . " Most immediate among our goals should be a fully participative if representative democracy, since agential functions are the genius of man. And we must also play up the gaining of that harmony of feeling and thought which bespeaks a life rich in values, and notably those social values which carry the spirit of the kinship of man. This is not to say that we should not be realistic. Hence the *second* prong of Sellars' two-way approach, e.g., the social sciences as factually diagnostic. In such a book as Robert Cooley Angell's *Free Society and Moral Crisis*, we have what I take to be the scientific approach to humanistic questions. Our values and conceptions must be specifically relevant to and documented by the actual human context. But as Sellars asserts and Angell likewise emphasizes, the social sciences "should have a keen eye for norms and the socially desirable." Such a two-way approach has the prospect of bringing to the fore goals, means and conditions. Only in such a setting, states Sellars, "can criteria of institutional evaluation increase in adequacy."[21]

The pathway of such progress is *a step by step matter*, an issue of sociological "due process." Sellars calls attention to "the slow process of diagnosis and therapeutics" disclosed in Falk's *Legal Order in a Violent World* and the brave attempt of Clark-Sohn at "a desirable reconstruction of the United Nations. One must, I suppose, mix pessimism with an appreciation of desirability as does Raymond Aron in his sociological and historical study of war and peace."[22]

The insights of men like Galbraith and Myrdal are indicative of the kind of steps that are essential to meeting the human requirements. We must, like Myrdal, distinguish between basic needs and other needs which can only be relatively satisfied. There must also be the proper balancing of the private and the public sectors. But such insights need elaboration and testing in the actual laboratory of experience. There is no substitute for either informed insights or for feedback from actual experience. Progress is cyclical. We can save ourselves a vast amount of repetition, however, through the study of history, but we shall need to be sure that the social patterns and conditions are sufficiently similar before we draw parallels.

Among the important flexibilities we need to develop are (1) the acceptance and appreciation of diverse styles of life within and without our own culture; (2) respect for and appreciation of other social patterns. Social pluralism is empirically realistic. Coexistence must become more than tolerance. Harmony and balance are essential social principles, and adequate dialogue is a condition for the operation of these principles. "Communication is the medium in fact within which humans live," both nationally and internationally.

In communication as in social transactions generally, there is no escaping the simple rule of gauging input by output and feedback. *Understanding* is built on the kinds of input which elicit desired and desirable outputs, and the human experience of desirabilities and undesirabilities is once again the test.

There is, in other words, no definitive formula for solving all social problems or even the basic ones. Not even John Dewey's problem-solving pattern is adequate to either the historical or philosophical dimensions of problems, though it is a working format. The test of social solutions is in their "satisfyingness" for the preponderance of people. The utilitarian formula of the greatest satisfaction for the greatest number is not enough; large minorities may thus be neglected. At the same time, to aim for well-being and satisfactoriness of life for everyone is at best directional. But we can all aim at a good life for the *preponderance* of people, inclusive of all groups. And it is a job for all, and not merely an affair of administration of some group of directors. It is also a job which calls for understanding.

But understanding is a huge task, and there are different levels of it. The most adequate level is a philosophical one, involving ontology, theory of knowledge, and the theory of value. Let us attempt to review what Sellars thinks is involved. There is more than social experience and practical aptitude; crossing the social divide involves a walk not through but in historical process. There is more than science, whether natural, behavioral, or formal, and more than religion however conceived. Each of these needs a philosophical completion, and all of them together comprise diverse but integrable perspectives. To understand men and their problems we need a well-grounded philosophy of man and his world, of the nature of his knowledge and the basis of the values he discriminates and espouses, of the conditions of his freedom and the agential meaning of freedom. (The word "freedom" is bandied about much too freely by Marcuse as well as by the vast majority of people. Sellars seems to me to suggest that by Marcuse's exceptional emphasis on freedom, he is condemning man to a second form of the non-dimensional life — an antithesis of the mechanistic man about whom he wrote one volume.) Social philosophy and social practice must therefore be built upon what seems redundant though it is not — i.e., a sufficiently realistic conception of reality. In other words, it must be built upon reliable knowing, and an adequate theory of reliable knowing, and on adequately documentable theories of man and his world and his values.

Yet anyone may be broadly and deeply informed and have a strong sense of human realities and of social processes, and of the self-corrections of his society. Whatever his perspective, there may be an openness to new information, new developments, new human needs, and constructive treatment of these.

"Society," states Sellars, "is in the making and not something finished. The alternatives are gradualism and revolution. But gradualism does not mean standing still." Gradualism requires constant revitalization and concern for "the concurrent dimensions of life."[23] But it saves mankind the loss of very hard-won gains.

Sellars closes with a warning: "The state is not an end in itself but a political instrument for adjusting means to ends. It may (1) move along rather unimaginatively in conventional grooves or (2) get out of hand through the hypertrophy of power to become a garrison state, or (3) face up to social problems in a participative way. The last is the only sane way but it requires a rather sane society. Here social patterns and political horizons meet."[24]

Sellars' projective social realism is a conception of a self-correcting society which has definitive human goals that entail the satisfyingness of life for every group and, so far as humanly possible, for every member of each group. Sellars starts from what has been achieved and goes on from there. He has no simple formula, only the ingredients of the process of social achievement and the philosophical groundwork for real achievement. But he is, thereby, well on his way across the great socio-personal divide with his goals consciously in sight.

Conclusion

Now may I, in conclusion, call attention to the fact that in crossing these several divides, Sellars has also crossed others, notably the divides between fact and values, between the sciences and the humanities. In actual living, fact and value are part and parcel of each other. As one of my students, Marilyn Maxwell, has pointed out, valuation for Sellars enters right into the process of perceiving. Locating and characterizing objects is an evaluative matter. Yet Sellars has distinguished clearly between cognizing and valuing. The effects of things on each other, which is the typical issue in knowing, is surely distinguishable from the roles things play in our patterns of life. There is a reflexiveness about valuation which we try to eliminate from the process of knowing per se. Knowing can, in other words, be dissociated from other interests, whereas these other interests are the preeminent factors in valuation. Values are the roles of objects in the human economy and function with reference to every type of interest or activity. At the same time, knowing is a conditioner of our interests and activities and thereby a modifier of values. We have thus a two-way relation between facts and values. Valuing goes beyond knowing to a realm of functional importances. And knowing, which is in one sense a kind of valuing, is a condition of reliable evaluations. There is no inherent opposition between them. There is simply a distinction of functions in a continuum.

As for the divide between science and the humanities, which has been so much stressed by C. P. Snow and other humanists, Sellars has shown their interconnection. In crossing each of the divides, and above all the socio-personal divide, Sellars has brought the humanities to bear upon the sciences and the sciences to bear on the humanities. In the process of living, and in thinking about issues of living, science and the humanities must and do come together. Our trouble is with our artificial dissections of human culture for special, generally professional, purposes. We become so absorbed in some one set of interests that we fail to see the relation of the parts to the whole. The functional wholeness of human living in terms of its culture brings science into the orbit of the humanities as a special and highly important set of both instruments and values.

Sellars' philosophy taken overall is thus an encompassing philosophy, epistemologically, ontologically, axiologically, and culturally. It is a philosophy of the human scene in its cosmic context. In "Objectives and Priorities," he writes:

> I see this little planet spinning in space and marvel at its history. This is not a story-book tale but one of struggle and tragedy and accomplishment. Stubbornness mixed with kindliness will achieve much but intelligence must

be added. Out of these ingredients should come wisdom. Thus I triangulate and extrapolate. It is obvious that I am concerned with participative democracy in the masses, and with the growth of international institutions. Patriotism is not enough. There must be resolutions of conflicts. And this is made possible by some openness of mind and by some recognition that it is tactically wise to agree to disagree, and wait on time.[25]

Notes and References

ABBREVIATIONS FOR BOOK AND PERIODICAL TITLES

CR	*Critical Realism*
EN	*Evolutionary Naturalism*
JP	*Journal of Philosophy*
NSR	*The Next Step in Religion*
PER	*Principles of Emergent Realism*
PPP	*Principles and Problems of Philosophy*
PPPP	*Principles, Perspectives and Problems of Philosophy*
PPR	*The Philosophy of Physical Realism*
PR	*Philosophical Review*
RCA	*Religion Coming of Age*
RAPW	*Reflections on American Philosophy from Within*
SPPH	*Social Patterns and Political Horizons*

Chapter One

1. Letter dated Nov. 11, 1971, from R. W. Sellars to the author. Quotations in this chapter, unless otherwise indicated, are from Sellars' unpublished "Biographical Remarks" and other written statements sent to the author.
2. Letter, Feb. 5, 1973, from R. W. Sellars.
3. George P. Adams and William Pepperell Montague, *Contemporary American Philosophy* (New York: Macmillan, 1930), II, 262.
4. "Critical Realism and the Time Problem I," and "Critical Realism and the Time Problem II," *Journal of Philosophy*, 5 (1908), 542 - 48; 597 - 602.
5. Célestin Bouglé, *The Evolution of Values*, translated by Helen Maude Sellars (New York: Henry Holt, 1920); reprinted New York: Augustus M. Kelley, 1970.
6. Quoted from the original manuscript of *Social Perspectives and Political Horizons* (Nashville: Aurora Press, 1970), pp. 473 - 44.
7. Samuel Alexander, "Natural Piety," *Hibbert Journal*, 1922.
8. Quoted from letter to the author dated Feb. 5, 1973.
9. "Critical Realism and its Critics," *Philosophical Review*, 33 (1924), 382.

10. J. E. Turner, "The Failure of Critical Realism," *Monist*, 32 (1922), 395 - 411.

11. "Sensations as Guides to Perceiving," *Mind*, 68, 269 (1959), 2 - 15; "Referential Transcendence," *Philosophy and Phenomenological Research* 22 (1961), 1 - 14; "Direct Referential Realism," *Dialogue*, 2 (1963), 135 - 43.

12. "A Clarification of Critical Realism," *Philosophy of Science* 6 (1939), 420.

13. In the MS of his *Critical Realism*, especially in Chapter IX: "Is Consciousness Alien to the Physical?"

14. Sellars, "Dewey on Materialism," *Philosophy and Phenomenological Research*, 3 (1942 - 43), 392.

15. Quoted from statement about Parker in Sellars' letter of Aug. 27, 1972.

16. D. H. Parker, "Some Comments on 'Reformed Materialism and Intrinsic Endurance,'" *Philosophical Review*, 53 (1944), 383 ff.

17. Quoted from statement in letter of August 27, 1972.

18. Yervant Krikorian, ed., *Naturalism and the Human Spirit* (New York: Columbia University Press, 1944).

19. Sidney Hook, "Is Physical Realism Sufficient?" *Ibid.*, pp. 544 - 551.

20. Ibid., p. 549.

21. "Reformed Materialism and Intrinsic Endurance," *Philosophical Review*, 53 (1944), 359 - 82.

22. R. W. Sellars, V. J. McGill, and Marvin Farber, *Philosophy for the Future: Quest of Modern Materialism* (New York: Macmillan, 1949).

23. Sellars lectured both at the University of Buffalo (now the State University of New York at Buffalo) and at the University of Pennsylvania. One symposium set up by Farber was on logical positivism with Bergmann of Iowa University.

24. *Critical Realism, Evolutionary Naturalism,* and *The Philosophy of Physical Realism,* (New York: Russell and Russell).

25. "Materialism and Relativity: A Semantic Analysis," *Philosophical Review*, 55 (1946), 25 - 51; "The Philosophy and Physics of Relativity," *Philosophy of Science*, 13 (1946), 177 - 95; "A Note on the Theory of Relativity," *Journal of Philosophy*, 43 (1946), 309 - 17.

26. According to Sellars, the concept of two observers in motion relative to each other is not the typical situation. Scientists are giving less and less attention to the factors of observers in relative motion. What we have typically is things, such as rods, in motion relationally to each other. The concept of relative motion is ambiguous. Relative motion is not a special kind of motion. All motion is inertial, with bodies moving relationally with respect to each other. Stating their motion in terms of the speed of light, the light will reach the front end of a relationally non-moving rod sooner than it will reach the front of a moving rod. But this does not mean that there is no such thing as absolute simultaneity. Should the rods overlap in their relation to a beam of light, the light will simultaneously reach a point on the moving rod that parallels the front of the unmoving rod.

Point of actual simultaneity

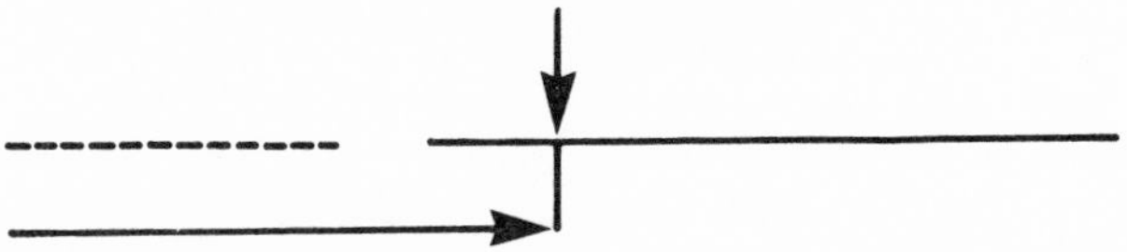

The physics of relativity can thus be stated in terms of inertial motion, without introducing a human equation and without the denial of absolute simultaneity. The mathematics is the same on a realistic basis as in the Einsteinian formulation. Compare Sellars statement in his Foreword, p.

27. Cf. *The New Scholasticism*, 45 (1971), No. 2, pp. 207 - 89.

Chapter Two

1. *George Santayana is the most obvious example. Charles A. Strong, J. B. Pratt, A. O. Lovejoy, A. K. Rogers, and Durant Drake were others; also D. C. Macintosh, who used the term "critical realism" as early as 1913.*
2. *Durant Drake is regarded as one of the more adequate exponents of critical realism.*
3. "*Consciousness and Conservation,*" *Journal of Philosophy*, 5 (1908), 238.
4. *Journal of Philosophy*, 7 (July, 1910), 393 - 401.
5. E. B. Holt, ed., *The New Realism* (New York: Macmillan, 1912).
6. W. P. Montague, "The Story of American Realism," in his *Ways of Things* (New York: Prentice-Hall, 1940), p. 235.
7. Among them were E. B. McGilvary and Arthur Murphy.
8. Montague, "The Story of American Realism," p. 251.
9. "Critical Realism and the Time Problem I," *Journal of Philosophy*, 5, (1908), 544 - 45. Hereafter cited as JP.
10. JP 5 (1908), 597 - 600.
11. *Critical Realism* (New York: Russell and Russell, 1969), p. 2. Hereafter cited as CR.
12. CR, Preface, p. ii.
13. Cf. Note 3.
14. CR, Preface, pp. ii and iii.
15. Montague, pp. 257 - 58.
16. *Philosophical Review*, 30 (1921), 482 - 93.
17. CR, Preface, p. iii.
18. CR, Preface, p. v.
19. CR, p. 275.
20. Montague, pp. 254 - 55.
21. Ibid.
22. Strong later abandoned the essence gambit.
23. "Direct Referential Realism," *Dialogue*, 2 (1963), 136.

24. *The Philosophy of Physical Realism* (New York: Russell and Russell, 1966), pp. 67 - 79. Hereafter cited as PPR.
25. "A Re-examination of Critical Realism," *Philosophical Review*, 38 (1929), 439 - 40.
26. Ibid., p. 140.
27. "A Clarification of Critical Realism," *Philosophy of Science*, 6 (1939), 415 ff. Read whole article for its use of "experience."
28. *Mind*, 68 (1959), 4.
29. PPR, p. vi.
30. "A Clarification of Critical Realism," *Philosophy of Science*, 6 (1939), 421.
31. R. W. Sellars, V. J. McGill, and Marvin Farber, *Philosophy for the Future: Quest of Modern Materialism* (New York: Macmillan, 1949), pp. 75 - 106.
32. "Realism, Naturalism, and Humanism," in G. P. Adams and W. P. Montague, eds., *Contemporary American Philosophy*, II, pp. 261 - 85.
33. *Reflections on American Philosophy from Within* (Notre Dame: University Press, 1969), p. 62.
34. Preston Warren, "American Realism 1900-1930, An Emerging Epistemology," *The Monist* (April, 1967).
35. *A Theory of Perception* (Princeton: Princeton University Press, 1971), p. 141.
36. PPR, p. 91.
37. Ibid., p. 84.
38. Ibid., p. 99.
39. "Causality and Substance," *Philosophical Review*, 52 (1943), 2.
40. *American Philosophy from Within*, p. 57.
41. "Accept the Universe as a Going Concern," *Religious Liberals Reply*, ed. by H. N. Wieman (Boston: Beacon Press, 1947), p. 172.

Chapter Three

1. In *Critical Realism* (New York: Russell and Russell, 1969), p. 253, Sellars states: "This solution of the mind-body problem opens up metaphysical vistas which I would gladly explore. But I must postpone this exploration until another time."
2. "Existentialism, Realistic Empiricism and Materialism," *Philosophy and Phenomenological Research*, 25, No. 3 (1965), p. 316.
3. "An Important Antinomy," *Psychological Review*, 15 (1908), 237 - 49; "Critical Realism and the Time Problem I," *Journal of Philosophy*, 5 (1908), 542 - 48. Hereafter cited as JP.
4. JP, 5, p. 545.
5. Ibid., pp. 545 - 46.
6. Ibid., pp. 545 - 46.
7. Ibid., p. 546.

8. "Causality," JP 6 (1909), 324.
9. Ibid., p. 325.
10. Ibid., p. 326.
11. Ibid.
12. Ibid.
13. "An Important Antinomy," *Psychological Review*, 15, p. 247.
14. James, *Principles of Psychology* (New York: Henry Holt, 1890), I, 149.
15. *Critical Realism*, p. 233.
16. Ibid.
17. Ibid., p. 229.
18. Ibid., p. 236.
19. *Evolutionary Naturalism* (Chicago: Open Court, 1922; reprinted, with Preface by T. A. Goudge and an Appendix by Lloyd Morgan, New York: Russell and Russell, 1969), p. 4. Hereafter cited as EN.
20. Ibid., p. 284.
21. Ibid., p. 296.
22. Ibid., pp. 297 - 334.
23. Ibid., p. 298.
24. Ibid., pp. 334 - 35.
25. JP, 54 (1957), 16, 485 - 93.
26. *Neglected Alternatives*, W. Preston Warren, ed. (Lewisburg, Pa.: Bucknell University Press, 1973).
27. *Philosophy and Phenomenological Research*, 20 (1959), 1, pp. 1 - 16.
28. Ibid., p. 6.
29. Ibid., p. 13.
30. "Why Naturalism and Not Materialism?" *Philosophical Review*, 36 (1927), 216 - 25. Hereafter cited as PR.
31. Notably in *Naturalism and the Human Spirit*, reviewed by Sellars in *Philosophy and Phenomenological Research*, 6 (1945 - 46), 436 - 39.
32. "Causality and Substance," PR, 52 (1943), 1 - 27. See Part 5 of article. Note that the term used is not *metaphysical* which etymologically means "beyond physics"; this begs the question. *Ontological* as a term does not prejudge the issue of whether there is a reality more ultimate than the physical.
33. *Principles, Perspectives, and Problems of Philosophy* (New York: Pageant Press, 1970). Hereafter cited as PPPP.
34. Ibid., p. 267. Quoted with the permission of the author and publisher. This applies also to Notes 35, 36, 37, 38, and 39.
35. These lines quoted from the manuscript of *Principles, Perspectives, and Problems of Philosophy* before publication and do not appear in the published volume.
36. Ibid., p. 265.
37. Ibid., pp. 265 - 66.
38. Ibid., p. 266.
39. Ibid., p. 267.

40. Ibid., p. 268.
41. Ibid., p. 273.
42. Ibid., p. 274.
43. PR, 52 (1943), 10.
44. PR, 53 (1944), 359 - 82.
45. "Some Comments on 'Reformed Materialism and Intrinsic Endurance,'" PR, 53 (1944), 383.
46. Ibid.
47. *Reflections on American Philosophy From Within* (Notre Dame: University Press, 1969), p. 116.

Chapter Four

1. *Principles, Problems, and Perspectives of Philosophy* (New York: Pageant Press, 1970), pp. 311 - 12. Quoted with the permission of the author and publisher.
2. *Journal of Philosophy*, 4 (1907), 14 - 18. Hereafter cited as JP.
3. JP 5 (1908), 235 - 38.
4. *The Psychological Review*, 15 (1908), 243, 248.
5. *The Psychological Review*, 14 (1907), 315 - 28.
6. "An Analytic Approach to the Mind-Body Problem," *Philosophical Review*, 47 (1938), 461. Hereafter cited as PR.
7. *Evolutionary Naturalism*, p. 286. Hereafter cited as EN.
8. "An Important Antinomy," *Psychological Review*, 15 (1908), 248 - 49.
9. "An Analytic Approach. . . ," PR, 47, p. 470.
10. CR, pp. 204 - 205.
11. Italics added.
12. *Aristotelian Society Proceedings*, n.s. 23 (1923), 61. Quoted with the permission of the author and publisher.
13. Ibid., pp. 56 - 57.
14. Ibid., p. 57.
15. EN, p. 295.
16. Ibid., p. 296.
17. CR, p. 208.
18. Ibid., p. 209.
19. Ibid., p. 210.
20. Ibid.
21. Ibid., pp. 210 - 11.
22. Ibid., p. 212.
23. Ibid.
24. Ibid., pp. 214 - 15.
25. Ibid., pp. 215 - 16.
26. Ibid., p. 219.
27. Ibid.
28. Ibid., p. 220.

29. Ibid.
30. Ibid., p. 221.
31. Ibid.
32. Ibid., p. 222.
33. Ibid., p. 226.
34. Ibid., p. 228.
35. Ibid., p. 236.
36. Read before the Aristotelian Society in London, 1922.
37. *Aristotelian Society Proceedings*, n.s. 23 (1923), 58 - 59. Quoted with the permission of the author and publisher.
38. Ibid., p. 59.
39. EN, p. 298.
40. "Sensations as Guides to Perceiving," *Mind*, 68 (1959), 12.
41. Cf. John O'Connor, *Modern Materialism: Readings on the Mind Body Identity* (New York: Harcourt Brace, 1969). Cf. also Norman Melchert, *Realism, Materialism and the Mind* (Springfield, Ill.: C. C. Thomas, 1968), pp. 187 - 89.
42. EN, p. 296.
43. "An Analytic Approach to the Mind-Body Problem," PR, 47 (1938), 478 - 81.
44. Ibid., p. 483.
45. Ibid., p. 484.
46. Ibid., pp. 467 - 68.
47. Ibid., p. 463.
48. Ibid., p. 476.
49. Ibid., p. 463.

Chapter Five

1. "Can a Reformed Materialism do Justice to Values," *Ethics*, 55 (1944), 35.
2. *Principles, Perspectives, and Problems of Philosophy* (New York: Pageant Press, 1970), p. 417. Hereafter cited as PPPP.
3. "A Naturalistic Theory of Value and Valuation," *Neglected Alternatives* (Lewisburg, Pa.: Bucknell Univ. Press, 1973), p. 349.
4. *The Philosophy of Physical Realism* (New York: Macmillan, 1932), Ch. XVII.
5. *Philosophy and Phenomenological Research*, 27 (1967), 1 - 16.
6. *Ethics*, 55 (1944), 27 - 45.
7. PR, 47 (1958), 243 - 51.
8. PPPP, p. 421.
9. Ibid., p. 424.
10. "Can A Reformed Materialism Do Justice to Values?" *Ethics*, 55 (1944), 34 - 35. Quoted with the permission of the author and publisher.
11. Ibid., p. 33.

12. Ibid., p. 35.
13. Ibid., p. 30.
14. Ibid., p. 31.
15. Ibid., p. 37.
16. Ibid., p. 45.
17. PPPP, pp. 433 - 36.
18. Ibid., p. 433.
19. Bernard Bosanquet, *Three Lectures on Aesthetics* (London: Macmillan, 1931), p. 3.
20. Ibid.
21. Laurence L. Buermeyer, *The Aesthetic Experience* (Merion, Pa.: The Barnes Foundation, 1924), pp. 89ff. (Cf. PPPP, p. 434.)
22. DeWitt H. Parker, *The Principles of Aesthetics* (New York: Silver Burdett and Co., 1920), p. 83.
23. PPPP, p. 435.
24. "You Shall Not Commit Adultery," *Readers Digest,* October, 1967.
25. PPPP, p. 380. Quoted with the permission of the author and publisher.
26. Ibid.
27. Ibid., p. 400.
28. Ibid., p. 403.

Chapter Six

1. "Undermining the Foundations," unpublished, p. 28.
2. "Naturalistic Humanism," *Religion in the Twentieth Century,* ed. by Vergilius Ferm (New York: Philosophical Library, 1948), p. 418.
3. Far Eastern religions are more naturalistic and thereby have a greater import than Western thinkers commonly acknowledge.
4. University of Notre Dame Press, 1969.
5. *The Next Step in Religion* (New York: Macmillan, 1918), p. 218. Hereafter cited as NSR.
6. Ibid., p. 1.
7. Ibid.
8. Ibid., pp. 1ff.
9. *Religion Coming of Age* (New York: Macmillan, 1928), p. 244. Hereafter cited as RCA.
10. NSR, p. 319.
11. RCA, p. 248.
12. Ibid., p. 250.
13. "Naturalistic Humanism," p. 417. Cf. Note 2.
14. Ibid., p. 422.
15. Ibid., p. 423.
16. "Humanist Manifesto," *The New Humanist,* 6, (1933) 3. Quoted with the permission of the author and publisher.
17. Ibid.

18. "Accept the Universe as a Going Concern," *Religious Liberals Reply*, ed. by H. N. Wieman (Boston: Beacon Press, 1947), pp. 171 - 72.
19. Cf. Note 11.
20. T. V. Smith, ed., *Philosophers Speak for Themselves*, (Chicago: University Press, 1934), p. 700.
21. Cf. Note 10.
22. PPR, pp. 449 - 50.
23. Sellars, *Reflections on American Philosophy from Within*, (Notre Dame: University Press, 1969), p. 172. Quoted with the permission of the author and publisher.
24. Ibid., p. 164.
25. Ibid., pp. 162 - 63.
26. Ibid., p. 173.
27. Ibid., p. 166 - 67.
28. Ibid., p. 165.
29. Ibid., p. 166.
30. Ibid., p. 173.
31. Ibid., p. 160.
32. "Humanism as a Religion," *Philosophy and Phenomenological Research*, 5 (1954), 96.

Chapter Seven

1. This phrasing is the author's.
2. "Social Philosophy and the American Scene," *Philosophy for the Future*, edited by R. W. Sellars, V. J. McGill, Marvin Farber (New York: Macmillan, 1949), p. 71.
3. W. P. Warren, ed., *Principles of Emergent Realism* (St. Louis: Warren H. Green Inc., 1970), pp. 273 - 75. Hereafter cited as PER.
4. Ibid.
5. Ibid., p. 15.
6. Ibid., pp. 20 - 22.
7. "Reason and Revolution," *Michigan Alumnus Quarterly Review*, 44, (1942), 212.
8. Ibid., p. 215.
9. PER, 301 - 02.
10. *Social Patterns and Political Horizons* (Nashville: Aurora Publishers, Inc., 1970) 216. Hereafter cited as SPPH.
11. Ibid., p. 190.
12. Letter from R. W. Sellars to the author, dated April 20, 1971.
13. Ibid.
14. *Experience and Nature*, (New York: Dover, 1958), 242.
15. *Inlander*, University of Michigan, 12 (1902), 258 - 59.
16. "Can A Reformed Materialism Do Justice to Values?" *Ethics* 55 (1944), 35.

17. Herbert Marcuse, *Negations* (Boston: Beacon Press, 1968), p. 81.
18. *Five Lectures* (Boston: Beacon Press, 1970), p. 83.
19. *Negations,* p. 43.
20. SPPH, p. 339.
21. Ibid., pp. 362 - 63.
22. Ibid., p. 363.
23. Ibid., p. 366.
24. Ibid., p. 373.
25. PER, p. 312.

Annotated Bibliography

The bibliography of Roy Wood Sellars' writing to 1954 was compiled by Gerald E. Myers for a Sellars symposium in *Philosophy and Phenomenological Research* (15, 1). It has since been updated by Norman Melchert in *Realism, Materialism and the Mind* and by Preston Warren in *Principles of Emergent Realism.* Sellars published two books and four essays since these updatings. The books, *Principles, Perspectives, and Problems of Philosophy* and *Social Patterns and Political Horizons,* are annotated in the first section below. The essays are: "A Possible Integration of Science and Philosophy," *Zygon* 4, (1969), 293 - 297; "Some Questions and Suggestions: An Expostulation," *Journal of Philosophy* 66 (1969), 859 - 60; and "Recollections of Marvin Farber," *Phenomenology and Natural Existence,* Dale Riepe, ed. (Albany: State University of New York Press, 1973). The fourth essay was a statement by Sellars in a series "Toward a New Humanist Manifesto" in *The Humanist* for January/February, 1973.

Because of the published bibliographies and other compilations of essays that are listed below, we are not here attempting to tabulate all articles or essays separately. We simply distinguish compiled and uncompiled topical groups of essays, and tabulate groups that are not yet compiled. Key essays on epistemology, ontology, philosophy of value, social philosophy and philosophy of religion have, for example, been compiled in my volume, *Principles of Emergent Realism;* and are not tabulated here. Among the topics on which papers have not yet been compiled are Reformed Materialism, the Philosophy of Science, and the Categories. We therefore list all published essays on these themes.

Most focal among Sellars' essays, whether compiled or otherwise, are: "Is There a Cognitive Relation?" *Journal of Philosophy,* 9 (1912); "The Double-Knowledge Approach to the Mind-Body Problem," *Aristotelian Society Proceedings,* n.s. 23, 1923; "Reformed Materialism and Intrinsic Endurance," *Philosophical Review,* 53, (1944); "Sensations as Guides to Perceiving," *Mind,* 68, (1959); and "Levels of Causality," *Philosophy and Phenomenological Research,* 20 (1959). Only two of these are referred to below.

PRIMARY SOURCES

1. Books by Sellars

Critical Realism. Chicago: Rand McNally, 1916; New York: Russell and Russell, with a new Preface, 1969. A study of the nature and conditions of knowledge with science as the model of human knowing yet inserted into and growing out of the realistic structure of experience.

The Next Step in Democracy. New York: Macmillan, 1916. A concern, in the name of a gradualistic kind of social programing, for the public sector of society.

The Next Step in Religion. New York: Macmillan, 1918. Historical religions are oriented prescientifically. The next step is to orient religion in terms of scientific humanism.

Evolutionary Naturalism. Chicago: Open Court, 1922; New York: Russell and Russell, with a Preface by T. A. Goudge, 1969. A first published volume on an emergent evolutionary cosmology, growing out of Sellars' thesis on the categories.

The Principles and Problems of Philosophy. New York: Macmillan, 1926. An introductory text in the light of the findings of science and in terms of a critical referential realism.

Religion Coming of Age. New York: Macmillan, 1928. An enlarged conception of the spiritual, and deepened conception of the natural, in a series on Philosophy for Laymen. Moot questions in religion are discussed in these terms.

The Philosophy of Physical Realism. New York: Macmillan, 1932; New York: Russell and Russell, with two added chapters, 1966. A systematic exposition of Sellars' basic philosophy, combining the epistemology of critical realism with the cosmology of emergent substantive naturalism. The mind-body problem is one of the key issues for this synthesis, together with the nature and status of values.

Philosophy for the Future: Quest of Modern Materialism. New York: Macmillan, 1949. A collaborative volume with Marvin Farber and V. J. McGill. Two of the essays are by R. W. Sellars, i.e., "Social Philosophy and the American Scene," and "Materialism and Human Knowing."

Lending a Hand to Hylas. Ann Arbor: Edwards Bros., 1968. With the help of a twentieth century scientific orientation and referential realism, Hylas turns the tables on Philonous. Sellars adds an Epilogue of 10 pages and a Prologue of 3½ pages.

Reflections on American Philosophy from Within. Notre Dame: University Press, 1969. A participant in the making of American philosophy critically examines men and movements of the twentieth century. British and Marxist thinkers and continental Existentialists are also encompassed.

Principles, Perspectives, and Problems of Philosophy. New York: Pageant Press, 1970. A complete revision of the 1926 *Principles and Problems* in the light of Sellars' later findings and formulations; hence, the most adequate systematic statement of his position. His theories of emergent evolution and perceptual knowledge are stated most clearly here.

Social Patterns and Political Horizons. Nashville: Aurora Press, 1970. Between *The Next Step in Democracy* (1916) and this volume in 1970, Sellars' writings on social philosophy were limited to three statements: "The Quality of Democracy," in the *Michigan Alumnus Quarterly Review* (1942); "Reason and Revolution," in the same quarterly in 1943, and "Social Philosophy and the American Scene," in *Philosophy for the Future* (1949). Now we have the fruition of Sellars' years of teaching and thought: his analysis of historically projected and/or attempted social systems from the Greeks to our twentieth-century isms; and his conclusions on what is involved in a constructive social realism.

Principles of Emergent Realism: Essays by Roy Wood Sellars, ed. Preston Warren. St. Louis: Warren H. Green, 1970. A compilation of key essays in epistemology, ontology, the mind-body relation, value theory, social philosophy, and philosophy of religion. All key essays listed in the introduction to this bibliography, except "Levels of Causality," are included in this edition.

Neglected Alternatives, ed. Preston Warren. Lewisburg, Pa.: Bucknell University Press, 1973. A volume of Sellars' critiques on Bradley, British theories of sense perception, Dewey, Lewis, Whitehead, Marxists, and Existentialists. Three constructive essays are included.

2. Contributions to books not otherwise listed

Essays in Critical Realism. London, 1920. Contributor of the chapter "Knowledge and its Categories." Pp. 187 - 219.

Philosophy Today, ed. Edward L. Schaub. Chicago and London, 1928. Contributor of the chapter "Current Realism." Pp. 19 - 36.

An Anthology of Recent Philosophy, ed. Daniel S. Robinson. New York, 1929. Contributor of the chapter "Current Realism" (reprinted from *Philosophy Today*). Pp. 279 - 90.

Contemporary American Philosophy, eds. G. P. Adams and W. P. Montague. New York, 1930. Contributor of the chapter "Realism, Naturalism, and Humanism." Vol. II, pp. 261 - 85.

The Development of American Philosophy, eds. W. G. Muelder and Laurence Sears. Cambridge, Mass., 1940. Contributor of the chapter "Knowledge and its Categories" (reprinted from *Essays in Critical Realism*). Pp. 431 - 40.

Religious Liberals Reply, ed. Henry Wieman. Boston, 1947. Contributor of the chapter "Accept the Universe as a Going Concern."

Philosophy for the Future, eds. R. W. Sellars, V. J. McGill and Marvin Farber. New York, 1949. Contributor of the chapters "Social Philosophy and the American Scene," pp. 61 - 75, and "Materialism and Human Knowing," pp. 75 - 106.

Philosophic Thought in France and the United States, ed. Marvin Farber. Buffalo, 1950. Contributor of the chapter "Critical Realism and Modern Materialism." Pp. 463 - 81.

A History of Philosophical Systems, ed. Vergilius Ferm. New York, 1950. Contributor of the chapter "The New Materialism." Pp. 418 - 428.

Religion in the Twentieth Century, ed. Vergilius Ferm. New York, 1948. Contributor of the chapter "Naturalistic Humanism." Pp. 415 - 431.

Evolution of Values, by Célestin Bouglé. Trans. by Helen Sellars. New York: Henry Holt, 1920. Preface by R. W. Sellars.

American Philosophy, ed. Ralph B. Winn. New York, 1950. Contributor of the chapter on "Realism." Pp. 193 - 202.

The Idea of War and Peace in Contemporary Philosophy, by Irving Louis Horowitz. Introductory essay by R. W. Sellars: "Philosophical Orientation and Peace." New York, 1957. Pp. vii - xx.

Realism, Materialism, and the Mind, by Norman Melchert. Foreword by R. W. Sellars. Springfield, Ill., 1968. Pp. vii - xiv.

Principles of Emergent Realism, ed. Preston Warren. Foreword by R. W. Sellars. St. Louis, 1970. Pp. v - ix.

Phenomenology and Natural Existence, ed. Dale Riepe. "Recollections of Marvin Farber" by R. W. Sellars. Albany, 1973.

"Toward a New Humanist Manifesto," by R. W. Sellars and ten others. *The Humanist,* January-February, 1973.

3. Uncompiled essays grouped by subject

Essays on materialism

"Dewey on Materialism," *Philosophy and Phenomenological Research,* 3 (1942), 381 - 92.

"Reformed Materialism and Intrinsic Endurance," *Philosophical Review,* 53 (1944), 359 - 82.

"Can A Reformed Materialism Do Justice to Values?" *Ethics,* 55 (1944), 28 - 45.

"Reflections on Dialectical Materialism," *Philosophy and Phenomenological Research,* 5 (1944 - 45), 157 - 79.

"Materialism and Relativity: A Semantic Analysis," *Philosophical Review,* 55 (1946), 25 - 51.

"Positivism and Materialism," *Philosophy and Phenomenological Research,* 7 (1946 - 47), 12 - 40.

"Materialism and Human Knowing," *Philosophy for the Future* (1949), pp. 75 - 106.

"Professor Goudge's Queries with Respect to Materialism," *Philosophical Review*, 60 (1951), 243 - 248.

Essays in the philosophy of science

"A Re-interpretation of Relativity," *Philosophical Review*, 41 (1932), 517 - 518.
"Positivism in Contemporary Philosophic Thought," *American Sociological Review*, 4 (1939), 26 - 42.
"Galileo Galilei," *Michigan Alumnus Quarterly Review*, 48 (1942), 301 - 307.
"Materialism and Relativity: A Semantic Analysis," *Philosophical Review*, 55 (1946), 25 - 51.
"The Philosophy and Physics of Relativity," *Philosophy of Science*, 13 (1946), 177 - 95.
"A Note on the Theory of Relativity," *Journal of Philosophy*, 43 (1946), 309 - 17.
"Positivism and Materialism," *Philosophy and Phenomenological Research*, 7 (1946 - 47), 12 - 40.
"Do the Natural Sciences Have Need of the Social Sciences?" *Philosophy of Science*, 15 (1948), 104 - 108.
"A Possible Integration of Science and Philosophy," *Zygon*, 4 (1969), 293 - 97.

Essays on the categories

"Critical Realism and the Time Problem," *Journal of Philosophy*, 5 (1908), 542 - 48 and 597 - 602.
"Space," *Journal of Philosophy*, 6 (1909), 617 - 23.
"Causality," *Journal of Philosophy*, 6 (1909), 323 - 28.
"A Thing and Its Properties," *Journal of Philosophy*, 12 (1915), 318 - 28.
"The Status of the Categories," *Monist*, 30 (1920), 220 - 39.
"Space and Time," *Monist*, 30 (1920), 321 - 64.
"Substance," *Mind*, 38 (1929), 473 - 88.
"Existence and Substance," *Journal of Philosophy*, 40 (1943), 197 - 208.
"Causality and Substance," *Philosophical Review*, 52 (1943), 1 - 27.
"Levels of Causality," *Philosophy and Phenomenological Research*, 20 (1959), 1 - 16.

Other uncompiled essays

"Re-interpretation of Democracy," *Inlander* (Univ. of Michigan Publication), 12 (1902), 252 - 61.
"The Nature of Experience," *Journal of Philosophy, Psychology, and Scientific Methods*, 4 (1907), 14 - 18.
"A Fourth Progression in the Relation of Body and Mind," *Psychological Review*, 14 (1907), 315 - 28.
"Professor Dewey's View of Agreement," *Journal of Philosophy, Psychology, and Scientific Methods*, 4 (1907), 432 - 35.

"On the Nature of Our Knowledge of the External World," *Philosophical Review*, 27 (1918), 502 - 12.
"An Approach to the Mind-Body Problem," *Philosophical Review*, 27 (1918), 150 - 63.
"The Epistemology of Evolutionary Naturalism," *Mind*, 28 (1919), 407 - 26.
"Evolutionary Naturalism and the Mind-Body Problem," *The Monist*, 30 (1920), 568 - 98.
"The Requirements of an Adequate Naturalism," *The Monist*, 31 (1921), 249 - 70.
"Is Consciousness Physical?" *Journal of Philosophy*, 19 (1922), 690 - 94.
"Concerning 'Transcendence' and 'Bifurcation'," *Mind*, 31 (1922), 31 - 39.
"Le Cerveau, L'âme et La Conscience," *Bulletin de la Société Francaise de Philosophie*, (January 18, 1923), 1 - 14.
"The Emergence of Naturalism," *International Journal of Ethics*, 34 (1924), 309 - 38.
"Critical Realism and its Critics," *Philosophical Review*, 33 (1924), 379 - 97.
"Cognition and Valuation," *Philosophical Review*, 35 (1926), 124 - 44.
"Current Realism in Great Britain and the United States," *The Monist*, 37 (1927), 503 - 20.
"Realism and Evolutionary Naturalism," *The Monist*, 37 (1927), 150 - 55.
"What is the Correct Interpretation of Critical Realism?" *Journal of Philosophy*, 24 (1927), 238 - 41.
"Why Naturalism and Not Materialism?" *Philosophical Review*, 36 (1927), 216 - 25.
"Critical Realism and Substance," *Mind*, 38 (1929), 473 - 88.
"A Re-examination of Critical Realism," *Philosophical Review*, 38 (1929), 439 - 55.
"A Naturalistic Interpretation of Religion," *The New Humanist*, 3, (1930), No. 4, 1 - 4.
"Humanism, Viewed and Reviewed," *The New Humanist*, 4 (1931) No. 15, 12 - 16.
"L'Hypothèse de l'Emergence," *Revue de Métaphysique et de Morale*, 40 (1933), 309 - 24.
"A Humanist Manifesto" [drafter and co-signer], *The New Humanist*, 6 (1933), No. 3.
"Religious Humanism," *The New Humanist*, 6 (1933), No. 3, 7 - 12.
"In Defense of the Manifesto," *The New Humanist*, 6 (1933), No. 6 6 - 12.
"Nature and Naturalism," *The New Humanist*, 7 (1934), No. 2, 1 - 8.
"George S. Morris," *Dictionary of American Biography*, 13 (1935), 208 - 209.
"Henry Philip Tappan," *Dictionary of American Biography*, 18 (1937), 302 - 303.
"Critical Realism and the Independence of the Object," *Journal of Philosophy*, 34 (1937), 541 - 50.

"A Clarification of Critical Realism," *Philosophy of Science*, 6 (1939), 412 - 21.
"Humanism as a Religion," *The Humanist*, 1 (1941), No. 1, 5 - 8.
"A Correspondence Theory of Truth," *Journal of Philosophy*, 38 (1941), 645 - 54.
"Aspects of Democracy II: The Quality of Democracy," *Michigan Alumnus Quarterly Review*, 48 (1942), 98 - 103.
"Causation and Perception," *Philosophical Review*, 53 (1944), 534 - 56.
"Does Naturalism Need Ontology?" *Journal of Philosophy*, 41 (1944), 686 - 94.
"Is Naturalism Enough?" *Journal of Philosophy*, 41 (1944), 533 - 44.
"Knowing and Knowledge," *Philosophy and Phenomenological Research*, 5 (1944 - 45), 341 - 44.
"Knowing Through Propositions," *Philosophy and Phenomenological Research*, 5 (1944 - 45), 348 - 49.
"The Meaning of True and False," *Philosophy and Phenomenological Research*, 5 (1944 - 45), 98 - 103.
"The Spiritualism of Lavelle and Le Senne," *Philosophy and Phenomenological Research*, 11 (1950 - 51), 386 - 93.
"Valuational Naturalism and Moral Discourse," *Philosophical Review*, 67 (1958), 243 - 51.
" 'True' as Contextually Implying Correspondence," *Journal of Philosophy*, 56 (1959), 18, 717 - 22.
"Panpsychism or Evolutionary Naturalism," *Philosophy of Science*, 27, 4 (1960), 329 - 50.
"American Realism: Perspective and Framework," in *Self, Religion, and Metaphysics: Essays in Memory of James Bissett Pratt*, ed. Gerald E. Myers. New York: Macmillan Co., 1961, 174 - 200.
"Referential Transcendence," *Philosophy and Phenomenological Research*, 22 (1961), No. 1, 1 - 14.
"Existentialism, Realistic Empiricism, and Materialism," *Philosophy and Phenomenological Research*, 25 (1965), No. 3, 315 - 32.
"In What Sense do Value Judgments and Moral Judgments have Objective Import?" *Philosophy and Phenomenological Research*, 25 (1967), No. 1, 1 - 16.
"In Defense of 'Metaphysical Veracity'," *The Philosophy of C. I. Lewis*, ed. Paul A. Schilpp. La Salle, Ill.: Open Court, 1968, 287 - 308.

SECONDARY SOURCES

BAHM, ARCHIE; FARBER, MARVIN; and TEN HOOR, MARTEN, editorial committee, "A Symposium in Honor of Roy Wood Sellars." *Philosophy and Phenomenological Research*, 15, 1, (1954), 1 - 103, with essays on: "Evolutionary Naturalism," by Archie Bahm; "Physical

Realism," by Wilfrid Sellars; "Critical Realism," by Roderick Chisholm; "The Mind-Body Problem," by John Kuiper; "Theory of Valuation," by William Frankena; and "Humanism as a Religion," by Marten Ten Hoor. Also a bibliography of Sellars' writings by Gerald E. Myers. Sellars wrote "A Rejoinder" in *Philosophy and Phenomenological Research,* 16, 1, (1955), 72 - 97.

BLAU, JOSEPH. *Men and Movements in American Philosophy.* New York: Prentice-Hall, 1952, treats the critical realism of Sellars on pages 293 - 301.

DELANEY, C. F. *Mind and Nature: A Study of the Naturalistic Philosophies of Cohen, Woodbridge, and Sellars.* South Bend and London: University of Notre Dame Press, 1969. Chapter V, 145 - 208, is on R. W. Sellars, "Mind as Organic Behavior." Chapters I, II, and VI relate to all three philosophers.

MELCHERT, NORMAN. *Realism, Materialism and the Mind.* Springfield, Ill.: C. C. Thomas, 1968. A sound treatment of Sellars' theory of knowledge, emergent materialism, and identity theory of the mind-body relation.

RECK, ANDREW. *Recent American Philosophy: Studies of Ten Representative Thinkers.* New York: Pantheon Books, 1962, elaborates the critical Realism of R. W. Sellars on 208 - 42.

The New Scholasticism. "Roy Wood Sellars Issue" presents a symposium in 1971 (45, 2) as follows: "The Realism of Roy Wood Sellars," by Andrew J. Reck; "Sellars and the Contemporary Mind-Body Problem," by C. F. Delaney; and "The Double-Knowledge Approach to the Mind-Body Problem," by Wilfrid Sellars.

WARREN, W. PRESTON. "Realism 1900 - 1930: An Emerging Epistemology," *Monist,* 51, 2, (1967), 179 - 205. Pp. 193 - 204 presents Sellars' development of the realistic epistemology.

———. "Foundations of Philosophy." *Bucknell Review,* 19, 3 (1972), 69 - 100. A comparison and contrast of Sellars' ontology with that of Heidegger and others.

———. "Experimentalism Plus." *Philosophy and Phenomenological Research,* 33, 2 (1972), 149 - 162. A juxtaposing of Sellars' cosmology to Dewey's methodology.

WERKMEISTER, W. H. *History of Philosophical Ideas in the United States.* New York: Ronald Press, presents Sellars' "Critical Realism," 446 - 52 and "Physical Realism," 486 - 93.

Index